SHADES OF GREEN

POEMS CHOSEN BY ANNE HARVEY

Shades of Green

ILLUSTRATED BY JOHN LAWRENCE

Greenwillow Books

NEW YORK

First published in Great Britain in 1991 by
Julia MacRae Books, an imprint of
the Random Century Group Ltd

First published in the United States in 1992
by Greenwillow Books

Printed in Great Britain
First American Edition
10 9 8 7 6 5 4 3 2 1

Library of Congress Cataloging-in-Publication Data
Shades of green / compiled by Anne Harvey :
pictures by John Lawrence.
    p.   cm.
Summary: A collection of nature poems grouped
in such categories as "The Grass Is Green," "He
Praises the Trees," and "Bird-world, Leaf-life."
ISBN 0-688-10890-3
1. Nature—Juvenile poetry.
2. Children's poetry, English.
3. Children's poetry, American.
4. Green—Juvenile poetry.
[2. Nature—Poetry.
2. English poetry—Collections. 3. American
poetry—Collections.]   I. Harvey, Anne.
II. Lawrence, John (date), ill.
PR1195.N3S5   1992
821.008'036—dc20
91-15234 CIP AC

CONTENTS

For ALAN MARTIN
at Pound House in Devon
where there is always poetry and where

'green and differences of green
and distances and depths of green
crown the cool gardens . . .'

with love

INTRODUCTION

Mid-July 1990 and my study floor is piled with poems for *Shades of Green*. Reading through the collection I am struck by the persistence of the word 'green'. It seems to leap out at me from almost every poem, and not only to describe leaves, grass, trees, moss, hedges . . . there's something else. Poets of all times have used green in a celebratory way to express hope and inspiration.

The end of July. Poems have now fallen into sections . . . grass, creatures, felling of trees, planting, flowers (and weeds). As always, when I think I've finished, a new idea arrives. A friend tells me of a twelfth century German nun, Hildegard of Bingen, who was probably the forerunner of today's Green Movement, which we think we started. She actually invented a word 'viriditas' meaning 'greening'. She believed in the intense power of all green life for our spiritual and physical well-being and her poetry, music and prayers are filled with this conviction. I am amazed to find that over eight hundred years ago Hildegard warned 'without nature humankind cannot survive' and wrote a poem that might easily have been written this year.

Now in the people
that were meant to green,
there is no more life of any kind.
There is only shrivelled barrenness.

The winds are burdened
by the utterly awful stink of evil,
selfish going-on.

Thunderstorms menace.

The air belches out
the filthy uncleanliness of the peoples.

There pours forth an unnatural,
a loathsome darkness,
that withers the green . . .

At different times in my life, green has been particularly important. When I was a child there was a tree in the fields behind our back garden that I liked to pretend was only mine. It wasn't an ordinary tree; there was a kind of presence there that couldn't be explained, mysterious, a little frightening, but not unpleasantly so. Now I think it might have had something to do with the Green Man, that ancient figure, part myth, part god, who appeared in various times and forms as a reminder of the power and force of nature. The Green Man has been known since the beginning of time, his origins are pagan, he is part of folklore. You can see stone sculptures and wood carvings of him in thousands of churches all over Europe, his wild hair and beard made from leaves, curling tendrils twining and snaking from mouth, nose and ears.

Many old inns and pubs are named The Green Man after him, and as Jack-in-the-Green he was the key figure in Spring rites, a tradition still popular in many areas. Caked with earth, layered with twigs and leaves, waving green boughs, he leads the dancers in Spring's Maytime triumph over Winter. The cold and dark days end, the green time returns; a time of renewal and hope, and in the Christian calendar, Resurrection after Death.

No poet described the Green Man more vividly than Charles Causley; or caught his underlying menace:

Green man in the garden
Staring from the tree,
Why do you look so long and hard
Through the pane at me?

Your eyes are dark as holly,
Of sycamore your horns,
Your bones are made of elder-branch,
Your teeth are made of thorns.

Your hat is made of ivy-leaf,
Of bark your dancing shoes,
And evergreen and green and green
Your jacket and shirt and trews.

Leave your house and leave your land
And throw away the key,
And never look behind, he creaked,
And come and live with me.

I bolted up the window,
I bolted up the door,
I drew the blind that I should find
The green man never more.

But when I softly turned the stair
As I went up to bed,
I saw the green man standing there.
Sleep well, my friend, he said.

vii

August 1990, and on holiday in Dorset and Devon I begin this introduction, inspired by the carvings of the Green Man in an old church. We walk through woods struck by the 1987 hurricanes and see new trees growing, and fallen trunks sprouting surprising growth – just like the trees in Ruth Pitter's poem, *Planting Mistletoe*.

So the tragic tree is the magic tree,
Running the whole range
Of growing and blowing
And suffering change,
Then buying, by dying,
The wonderful and strange . . .

Storms and wars destroy, but vegetation will return. After the destruction by bombing in the Second World War, weeds and wild flowers crept through cracks in stone and brick, rosebay willowherb, dandelions . . . the Green Man again?

And now, when scientific and industrial development has almost gone too far, he returns, his message, tumbling in green leaves from his mouth,

Annihilating all that's made
To a green thought in a green shade.

ANNE HARVEY

A Green Hope

WHAT IS GREEN?

Green is the grass
And the leaves of trees
Green is the smell
Of a country breeze . . .

Green is a coolness
You get in the shade
Of the tall old woods
Where the moss is made.

Green is a flutter
That comes in Spring
When frost melts out
Of everything.
Green is a grasshopper
Green is jade
Green is hiding
In the shade –
Green is an olive
And a pickle.
The sound of green
Is a water-trickle.
Green is the world
After the rain
Bathed and beautiful
Again . . .

Green is the meadow,
Green is the fuzz
That covers up
Where winter was.
Green is ivy and
Honeysuckle vine.
Green is yours
Green is mine . . .

Mary O'Neill

WHEN MY BABY LOOKS AT TREES

When my baby looks at trees he sees
the wind's shape;
his face becomes still
as the branches sway and dip
for his delight, as the bright
sky dances through. He stares,
his nose twitches at leaf
and resin, sour bark, sweet earth,
the juices in the wood.

If he could climb trees
he'd be out of my arms and up
in the creaking heights
laughing among the leaves;
and his white hands move jerkily
trying to touch. What he sees
is the glow of the sap as it spreads
out and upwards, the shine
of the tree's breath.

His eyes widen and darken
and lighten to green;
a smile brushes his mouth
and cheek, and a look
passes light between him and the tree.
He is close in my arms, but apart.
When we turn to go
his skin smells of forests, he holds
his face to the wind.

Hilary Llewellyn-Williams

THE GREEN SPRING

When Spring comes
I see the woods turning green,
The water in the river turning green,
The hills turning green,
The beetles turning green,
And even the white-bearded old man turning green.
The green blood
Nurtures the fatigued earth,
And from the earth bursts forth
A green hope.

Shan-Mei

Why are the green hills always so green?
Why do streams run day and night in a ceaseless flow?
We too then unceasing, will remain forever green.

Yi-Hwang

THE GREEN PLEASURE

There is this green pleasure
Of shelling the first peas –
The gentle thumb-press
At the top till they split open
Revealing those small pearls,
Sweet and crisp for quick cooking.

Each summer I look forward
To their lips parting
With a mild pop, air escaping
From the still young pods
And watch the pot filling
With each green promise.

Lotte Kramer

I ASKED THE LITTLE BOY WHO CANNOT SEE

I asked the little boy who cannot see,
'And what is colour like?'
'Why, green,' said he,
'Is like the rustle when the wind blows through
The forest; running water, that is blue;
And red is like a trumpet sound; and pink
Is like the smell of roses; and I think
That purple must be like a thunderstorm;
And yellow is like something soft and warm;
And white is a pleasant stillness when you lie
And dream.'

Anon

LINES WRITTEN IN EARLY SPRING

I heard a thousand blended notes,
While in a grove I sate reclined,
In that sweet mood when pleasant thoughts
Bring sad thoughts to the mind.

To her fair works did Nature link
The human soul that through me ran;
And much it grieved my heart to think
What man has made of man.

Through primrose tufts, in that green bower,
The periwinkle trailed its wreaths;
And 'tis my faith that every flower
Enjoys the air it breathes.

The birds around me hopped and played,
Their thoughts I cannot measure:–
But the least motion which they made,
It seemed a thrill of pleasure.

The budding twigs spread out their fan,
To catch the breezy air;
And I must think, do all I can,
That there was pleasure there.

If this belief from heaven be sent,
If such be Nature's holy plan,
Have I not reason to lament
What man has made of man?

William Wordsworth

EVENING OVER THE FOREST

Watch.
What is it you see?

The stark bough of an oak.
Beyond it the evening sky.
Clear, clear the evening sky
And green like a green pearl.

Did you hear?
What did you hear?

The harsh cry of a bird,
Beyond the evening sky.
Still, still the evening sky
And green like a green pearl.

Oh, search.
What is it you see?

Fiery snowy little cloud
Sailing to sleep in the sky.
Dim, dim the evening sky
Like a deep green pearl.

Come away.
Come away.

Beatrice Mayor

from LEAVES OF GRASS

There was a child went forth every day,
And the first object he looked upon that object he became,
And that object became part of him for the day or a certain part of
      the day . . . or for many years or stretching cycles of years.

The early lilacs became part of this child,
And grass, and white and red morning glories, and white and red
      clover, and the song of the phoebe-bird . . .

And the appletrees covered with blossoms, and the fruit afterward
      . . . and woodberries . . . and the commonest weeds by the road.

Walt Whitman

Rings of Grain

THE TREES

The trees are coming into leaf
Like something almost being said;
The recent buds relax and spread,
Their greenness is a kind of grief.

Is it that they are born again
And we grow old? No, they die too.
Their yearly trick of looking new
Is written down in rings of grain.

Yet still the unresting castles thresh
In fullgrown thickness every May.
Last year is dead, they seem to say,
Begin afresh, afresh, afresh.

Philip Larkin

TO LOOK AT ANYTHING

To look at anything,
If you would know that thing,
You must look at it long:
To look at this green and say
'I have seen spring in these
Woods,' will not do – you must
Be the thing you see:
You must be the dark snakes of
Stems and ferny plumes of leaves,
You must enter in
To the small silences between
The leaves,
You must take your time
And touch the very peace
They issue from.

John Moffitt

from A SHROPSHIRE LAD

Loveliest of trees, the cherry now
Is hung with bloom along the bough,
And stands about the woodland ride
Wearing white for Eastertide.

Now, of my threescore years and ten,
Twenty will not come again,
And take from seventy springs a score,
It only leaves me fifty more.

And since to look at things in bloom
Fifty springs are little room,
About the woodlands I will go
To see the cherry hung with snow.

A.E. Housman

THE STRICKEN MAGNOLIA

These, that were chalices,
Are sheets:
These, that were clouds,
Are a carpet:
These, that were parts,
Are a whole:
This, that was flowers,
Is light.

Bryan Guinness

PETALS

Last night's wind has blown off all the peach blossoms in the garden.
Child, you want to sweep the flowers away:
Aren't the fallen petals flowers?
   Why not leave them alone?

Anon

THE MAPLE TREE

The Maple with its tassell flowers of green
That turns to red, a stag horn shapèd seed
Just spreading out its scallopped leaves is seen,
Of yellowish hue yet beautifully green.
Bark ribb'd like corderoy in seamy screed
That farther up the stem is smoother seen,
Where the white hemlock with white umbel flowers
Up each spread stoven to the branches towers
And mossy round the stoven spread dark green
And blotched leaved orchis and the blue-bell flowers –
Thickly they grow and neath the leaves are seen.
I love to see them gemm'd with morning hours.
I love the lone green places where they be
And the sweet clothing of the Maple tree.

John Clare

THE OLD ONES

In the May evening
Flowing with golden light,
Out went the old woman
To meditate;

Pottered through the orchard,
Her cat at her side –
So old the two of them,
Time they died.

But when they sat them down on the bench
Under an apple tree,
'Here we are,' said the old woman,
'Where we belong to be.'

Blossom floated from the branches,
Light as snowflakes touched those two friends,
Coarsened fur and faded hair
And bent transparent hands.

So they sat, the two of them,
In some content . . .
The violent bats swerved to and fro,
The brightness went,

Leaving the sky as any shell
Delicate and pure;
Soundless flitted past the moths
Through the dim blossomy air.

Yet still, still, those old ones –
As if the sun still shone –
Sat there, never noticing
Another day had gone.

'Here we are,' said the old woman,
'Under the apple tree
'On this sweet May evening,
'Where we belong to be.'

Frances Bellerby

IN THE MOUNTAINS ON A SUMMER DAY

Gently I stir a white feather fan,
With open shirt sitting in a green wood.
I take off my cap and hang it on a jutting stone;
A wind from the pine-tree trickles on my bare head.

Li Po

SUMMER RAIN

Summer rain falling all afternoon,
Turning the trees to green mist,
Soaking the railway cutting rhododendrons.
A frill of raindrops on their drenched mauve petals,
And the laurels water-polished.

And over the bridge go the blue-skirted schoolgirls,
With a twinkling of white ankle socks,
Their straw hats tilted to the summer rain.

David Sutton

AUGUST AT HOME

How rich the elms, and large, and summer-sad,
    My childhood trees;
I thought of them as people, when I had
    No words for them like these.
I drink their presence, and I go my ways,
    They bring no altered mood;
These heavy trees are part of all my days,
    Like sleep they are, and food.

Frances Cornford

THE LITTLE GREEN ORCHARD

Some one is always sitting there,
      In the little green orchard;
  Even when the sun is high,
  In noon's unclouded sky,
  And faintly droning goes
  The bee from rose to rose,
Some one in shadow is sitting there,
      In the little green orchard.

Yes, and when twilight's falling softly
      On the little green orchard;
  When the grey dew distils
  And every flower-cup fills;
  When the last blackbird says,
  'What–what!' and goes her way–ssh!
I have heard voices calling softly
      In the little green orchard.

Not that I am afraid of being there,
      In the little green orchard;
  Why, when the moon's been bright,
  Shedding her lonesome light,
  And moths like ghosties come,
  And the horned snail leaves home:
I've sat there, whispering and listening there,
      In the little green orchard;

Only it's strange to be feeling there,
          In the little green orchard;
     Whether you paint or draw,
     Dig, hammer, chop, or saw;
     When you are most alone,
     All but the silence gone . . .
Some one is waiting and watching there,
          In the little green orchard.

Walter de la Mare

Green, I love you green. Green wind.
     Green branches.

Federico García Lorca

THE ELM

This is the place where Dorothea smiled.
I did not know the reason, nor did she.
But there she stood, and turned, and smiled at me:
A sudden glory had bewitched the child.
The corn at harvest, and a single tree.
This is the place where Dorothea smiled.

Hilaire Belloc

AUTUMN

Summer, the shining one, is tarnished and rusted;
The sun-silvered leaves are corroded and fallen,
The shining hopes, little by little,
Dulled.
A small black wind
Angrily churns the leaves;
Autumn is on us;
Soon winter.

Gerda Mayer

LEAVES IN THE YARD

Leaves have the lightest footfall
Of all who come in the yard.
They play rounders, they play tig,
They play no-holds-barred.

Late, when people are all asleep
Still they scamper and weave.
They play robbers, they play cops,
They play Adam-and-Eve.

Tap, tap, on the pavement,
Flit, flit, in the air:
The sentry-going bat wonders what they're at,
The blank back-windows stare.

When they rest, the wind rests;
When they go, he goes too;
They play tiptoe, they play mouse,
He shouts *hoo*.

Summer, they fidgeted on trees,
Then autumn called 'Enough!'
They play leapfrog, they play fights,
They play blind-man's-buff.

Ragged, swept in corners,
Fallen beyond recall,
Ragged and old, soon to be mould, –
But light of heart wins all.

Hal Summers

IN HARDWOOD GROVES

The same leaves over and over again!
They fall from giving shade above,
To make one texture of faded brown
And fit the earth like a leather glove.

Before the leaves can mount again
To fill the trees with another shade,
They must go down past things coming up.
They must go down into the dark decayed.

They *must* be pierced by flowers and put
Beneath the feet of dancing flowers.
However it is in some other world
I know that this is the way in ours.

Robert Frost

THE LEAVES ARE DOWN

The leaves are down from all but the cherry now.
The lawn grows autumn toadstools, fog falls, a frost,
the dark house gapes, the clocks go back, but
the cherry holds its leaves, refusing to believe in winter
even now.

Sean Street

TREE IN WINTER

Not at Home to Callers
Says the Naked Tree –
Bonnet due in April –
Wishing you Good Day –

Emily Dickinson

WRITTEN IN SURREY

My skinny little cherry tree
   alighting without sound
like a feather fallen from
   a cloud to the ground,
you shake, as you shiver there
   bare in the white day
birds out of your nested hair
   and like memories they
grow dark in the evening air
   as they sweep away.
But once above your aery house
   the sun of the blue day
hung among your golden boughs
   and saw the children play
and the summer saunter by
   trailing her hand in the auburn
cornfield of July.
   O skinny little cherry tree
all the memories pass.
   What is the image that you see
shed on the frosty grass?
   Where once on a summer time
lovers and children stood
   an old man without a scythe
gathering up wood.

George Barker

THE SONG OF THE FIR

There was a fir
Within a wood,
  Far away, far away:
It stands no longer where it stood.
Dance around the tree to-day.

It had a scent
Made sweet the air,
  Far away, far away:
The sweetness is no longer there.
Breathe the sweetness as you play,
And dance around the tree to-day.

It grew between
The earth and sky,
  Far away, far away:
The tree has lost its liberty
And between four walls must stay.
Breathe the sweetness as you play,
And dance around the tree to-day.

On its tip
It bore a cone,
  Far away, far away:
Now that simple fruit is gone
Hang the tree with presents gay
Mid the walls where it must stay,
Shedding sweetness where you play,
And dance around the tree to-day.

Eleanor Farjeon

THE BEECH TREE

From the top window
    I can see
a long garden
    and a beech tree.

Three months ago
    the autumn came
and lit the branches
    like a flame.

In January,
    overnight,
the beech burst into
    blazing white.

Another year
    and I will see
the red-hot
    and the white-hot tree.

But there will be
    a spring between
and it will turn
    the embers green.

The red light stopped it.
    White was slow.
But the green makes
    the summer go.

Conor Carson

TRAFFIC LIGHT

This smoky winter morning –
   do not despise the green jewel shining among the twigs
   because it is a traffic light.

Charles Reznikoff

THAW

Over the land freckled with snow half-thawed
The speculating rooks at their nests cawed
And saw from elm-tops, delicate as flower of grass,
What we below could not see, Winter pass.

Edward Thomas

The Grass is Green

BAREFOOT

After that tight
Choke of sock
And blunt
Weight of shoe,

The foot can feel
Clover's green
Skin
Growing,

And the fine
Invisible
Teeth
Of gentle grass,

And the cool
Breath
Of the earth
Beneath.

Valerie Worth

SPRING SONG

Out into the garden below me
came a little boy,
say five or six, in scarlet trousers;
and the sun shone on his face,
and the wind blew up his hair,
and he jumped up and down
on the grass-green grass.
He was joined by a miniature poodle
curly and wild, springily sprung,
and it too went jumping about
on the grass-green grass.

And it looked such fun
what with the daffodils and the sun
what with the pink on the almond trees
and the fierce breeze
and the boy larking
and the dog barking
that I thought I would jump too.
It was the obvious thing to do.

So the boy and the poodle jumped up and down
on the grass-green grass,
and I jumped up and down
on my best Bukhara rug,
and the gouache of Epping Forest by Epstein
fell off the wall,
and the photograph of the Dowager Lady Reading
fell off the desk,
and 'Bliss' by Katherine Mansfield
fell off its shelf,

and a monstrous piece of plaster
fell off the ceiling,
and my whole world spun
in a whirl of whizzing black spots
as shouting great shouts of praise
to the glorious spring
I fell to the floor.

Visiting hours, by the way, are from four to six.

Virginia Graham

HILL ROLLING

I kind of exploded inside,
and joy shot out of me.
I began to roll down the grassy hill.
I bent my knees up small, took a deep breath
and I was off.
My arms shot out sideways.
I gathered speed.
My eyes squinted
Sky and grass, dazzle and dark.

I went on forever,
My arms were covered with dents,
holes, squashed grass.
Before I knew it I was at the bottom.
The game was over.
The door of the classroom closed behind me.
I can smell chalk dust, and hear the voice of teacher,
to make me forget my hill.

Andrew Taylor

A CHILD SAID 'WHAT IS THE GRASS?'

A child said 'What is the grass?' fetching
        it to me with full hands;
How could I answer the child? I do not
        know what it is any more than he.

Walt Whitman

THE PLEASURES OF FRIENDSHIP

The pleasures of friendship are exquisite,
How pleasant to go to a friend on a visit!
I go to my friend, we walk on the grass,
And the hours and moments like minutes pass.

Stevie Smith

DOWN BY THE RIVER

Walking through the long grass
on our way to the river,
my son wanders ahead, hunting
imaginary lions, happy
and contented in his game.
The day is closing down,
storm clouds gathering,
and a fresh breeze
ripples across the fields
from the sea.
       A jet-plane
screams through the air, and
the child comes running,
clutching my hand, and pulling
his hood up as the wind
whips through the grass.
The rain starts to fall,
and as we stand on the river bank
I look at the dark clouds overhead.

Jim Burns

GAZELLE

O gaze on the graceful gazelle as it grazes,
It grazes on green growing leaves and on grass.
On grasses it grazes, go gaze as it passes,
It passes so gracefully, gently, O gaze!

Mary Ann Hoberman

FOUR DUCKS ON A POND

Four ducks on a pond,
A grass bank beyond,
A blue sky of spring,
White clouds on the wing;
What a little thing
To remember for years –
To remember with tears.

William Allingham

GREENING

I am the breeze that nurtures all things green,
I encourage blossoms to flourish with ripening fruits.
I am the rain coming from the dew
that causes the grasses to laugh
with the joy of life.

Hildegard of Bingen

What is green? the grass is green
With small flowers between . . .

Christina Rossetti

GRASS

Grass on the lawn
Says nothing:
Clipped, empty,
Quiet.

Grass in the fields
Whistles, slides,
Casts up a foam
Of seeds,

Tangles itself
With leaves: hides
Whole rustling schools
Of mice.

Valerie Worth

THE GRASSES

The grasses nod together
  In the field where I play,
And I can never quite catch
  What they whisper and say.
Sometimes their talk
  Seems friendly and wise,
Sometimes they speak of me
With gossip and lies.

James Reeves

from THE ELEMENTS OF DRAWING

Gather a simple blade of grass
    and examine it for a moment, quietly,
its narrow sword-shaped strip of fluted-green.
Think of it well and judge whether there
    be any man so deeply loved,
    by God so highly graced
    as that narrow strip of green . . .

John Ruskin

I THINK

I will write you a letter,
June day. Dear June Fifth,
you're all in green, so
many kinds and all one
green, tree shadows on
grass blades and grass
blade shadows. The air
fills up with motor
mower sound. The cat
walks up the drive
a dead baby rabbit
in her maw. The sun
is hot, the breeze
is cool. And suddenly
in all the green
the lilacs bloom,
massive and exquisite
in colour and shape
and scent. The roses
are more full of
buds than ever. No
flowers. But soon.
June day, you have
your own perfection
so green to say
goodbye to. Green,
stick around
a while.

James Schuyler

NEW SAYING

A lawn, a lily
　　And a lilac tree:
They takes a lot of beating
　　Wherever they be.

Reginald Arkell

SUNDAY

The mint bed is in
bloom: lavender haze
day. The grass is
more than green and
throws up sharp and
cutting lights to
slice through the
plane tree leaves. And
on the cloudless blue
I scribble your name.

James Schuyler

He Praises the Trees

THE GREEN GRASS GROWING ALL AROUND

There was a tree stood in the ground,
The prettiest tree you ever did see;
The tree in the wood, and the wood in the ground,
And the green grass growing all around.
And the green grass growing all around.

And on this tree there was a limb,
The prettiest limb you ever did see;
The limb on the tree, and the tree in the wood,
The tree in the wood, and the wood in the ground,
And the green grass growing all around.
And the green grass growing all around.

And on this limb there was a bough,
The prettiest bough you ever did see;
The bough on the limb, and the limb on the tree,
The limb on the tree, and the tree in the wood,
The tree in the wood, and the wood in the ground,
And the green grass growing all around.
And the green grass growing all around.

Now on this bough there was a nest,
The prettiest nest you ever did see;
The nest on the bough, and the bough on the limb,
The bough on the limb, and the limb on the tree,
The limb on the tree, and the tree in the wood,
The tree in the wood, and the wood in the ground,
And the green grass growing all around.
And the green grass growing all around.

And in the nest there were some eggs,
The prettiest eggs you ever did see;
Eggs in the nest, and the nest on the bough,
The nest on the bough, and the bough on the limb,
The limb on the tree, and the tree in the wood,
The tree in the wood, and the wood in the ground,
And the green grass growing all around.
And the green grass growing all around.

Anon

OBSERVING

That tree across the way
Has been a magnet to me all this year.
What happens to it is what interests me.
I've watched a blackbird stay
Glued for a moment, unglue, disappear.
Violence came in April to that tree,
Made its whole being sway

Till I was sure it could
Not stand, would snap and in torn fragments lie,
Leaving another entrance for the sky.
But that frail-seeming wood,
A conifer with intricate small leaves,
Stands under stars now while a new moon conceives
Itself before the eye.

Elizabeth Jennings

TREE AT MY WINDOW

Tree at my window, window tree,
My sash is lowered when night comes on;
But let there never be curtain drawn
Between you and me.

Vague dream-head lifted out of the ground,
And thing next most diffuse to cloud,
Not all your light tongues talking aloud
Could be profound.

But tree, I have seen you taken and tossed,
And if you have seen me when I slept,
You have seen me when I was taken and swept
And all but lost.

That day she put our heads together,
Fate had her imagination about her,
Your head so much concerned with outer,
Mine with inner, weather.

Robert Frost

TREES

The Birch is a fountain.
The Willow's a bower.
The Elm is a mountain.
The Poplar's a tower.
The Chestnut's a chapel.
The Aspen's a song.
The house of the Apple holds right things and wrong.

The Cedar's a table.
The Maple's a flame.
The Fir-tree's a fable.
The Mulberry's a game.
The Beech is a ceiling.
The Pine is a mast.
The Oak has the feeling of first things and last.

Eleanor Farjeon

I think that I shall never see
A poem as lovely as a tree,
Poems are made by fools like me
But only God can make a tree.

Alfred (Joyce) Kilmer

HE PRAISES THE TREES

Huge-headed oak,
you are tall, tall.
Small hazel, pick
me your secret nuts.

Alder, friendly one,
gleam, shine;
you bar no gap
with a toothed thorn.

Blackhorn, dark one,
provide sloes;
watercress, brim
the blackbirds' pools.

Small one, pathway
loiterer, green
leaved berry, give me
your speckled crimson.

Apple tree, let me
shake you strongly.
Rowan, drop me
your bright blossom.

Briar, relent.
Your hooks have fed
content till you
are filled with holy blood.

Church Yew, calm
me with grave talk.
Ivy, bring dream
through the dark wood.

Hollybush, bar me
from winter winds.
Ash, be a spear
in my fearful hand.

Birch, oh blessed
birch tree, sing
proudly the tangle
of the wind.

Robin Skelton

THE PRAYER OF THE TREE

You who pass by and would raise your hand
 against me, hearken ere you harm me,
I am the heat of your hearth on the cold
 winter night, the friendly shade screening
 you from summer sun,
And my fruits are refreshing draughts
 quenching your thirst as you journey on.
I am the beam that holds your house, the
 board of your table, the bed on which you
 lie, the timber that builds your boat.
I am the handle of your hoe, the door of your
 homestead, the wood of your cradle,
 the shell of your last resting place.
I am the gift of God and the friend of man.
You who pass by, listen to my prayer and
 Harm me not.

Anon

HIS OWN COUNTRY

I shall go without companions,
  And with nothing in my hand;
I shall pass through many places
  That I cannot understand –
Until I come to my own country,
  Which is a pleasant land!

The trees that grow in my own country
  Are the beech tree and the yew;
Many stand together,
  And some stand few.
In the month of May in my own country
  All the woods are new.

When I get to my own country
  I shall lie down and sleep;
I shall watch in the valleys
  The long flocks of sheep.
And then I shall dream, for ever and all,
  A good dream and deep.

Hilaire Belloc

RAINFOREST

The forest drips and glows with green.
The tree-frog croaks his far-off song.
His voice is stillness, moss and rain
drunk from the forest ages long.

We cannot understand that call
unless we move into his dream,
where all is one and one is all
and frog and python are the same.

We with our quick dividing eyes
measure, distinguish and are gone.
The forest burns, the tree-frog dies,
yet one is all and all are one.

Judith Wright

FOR FOREST

Forest could keep secrets
Forest could keep secrets

Forest tune in everyday
to watersound and birdsound
Forest letting her hair down
to the teeming creeping of her forest-ground

But Forest don't broadcast her business
no Forest cover her business down
from sky and fast-eye sun
and when night come
and darkness wrap her like a gown
Forest is a bad dream woman

Forest dreaming about mountain
and when earth was young
Forest dreaming of the caress of gold
Forest rootsing with mysterious eldorado

and when howler monkey
wake her up with howl
Forest just stretch and stir
to a new day of sound

but coming back to secrets
Forest could keep secrets
Forest could keep secrets
        And we must keep Forest

Grace Nichols

from A SHROPSHIRE LAD

On Wenlock Edge the wood's in trouble;
   His forest fleece the Wrekin heaves;
The gale, it plies the saplings double,
And thick on Severn snow the leaves.

'Twould blow like this through holt and hanger
   When Uricon the city stood:
'Tis the old wind in the old anger,
   But then it threshed another wood.

Then, 'twas before my time, the Roman
   At yonder heaving hill would stare:
The blood that warms an English yeoman,
   The thoughts that hurt him, they were there.

There, like the wind through woods in riot,
   Through him the gale of life blew high;
The tree of man was never quiet:
   Then 'twas the Roman, now 'tis I.

The gale, it plies the saplings double,
   It blows so hard, 'twill soon be gone:
To-day the Roman and his trouble
   Are ashes under Uricon.

A.E. Housman

WORDS

In woods are words.
You hear them all,
Winsome, witless or wise,
When the birds call.

In woods are words.
If your ears wake
You hear them, quiet and clear,
When the leaves shake.

In woods are words.
You hear them all
Blown by the wet wind
When raindrops fall.

In woods are words
Kind or unkind;
Birds, leaves and hushing rain
Bring them to mind.

James Reeves

TWO TREES

I saw where a crab-apple tree grew through a willow,
That was old and rotten, hanging above the river.
Its small lithe trunk matched perfectly a hollow
In the other's side; it clung there like a lover,
And all its branches were so twined around
And through the willow's branches, one could say
Only by tracing both trunks to the ground
Which was the loveliness, which the decay.
And yet if the decay should die at last,
So should the loveliness be sure to follow
From having clung to it so long, so fast.
It was the crab that chose this way to grow,
It was the crab gave sweetness to the air.
The willow played its part, by standing there.

David Sutton

WEEPING WILLOW IN MY GARDEN

My willow's like a frozen hill
Of green waves, when the wind is still;
But when it blows, the waves unfreeze
And make a waterfall of leaves.

Ian Serraillier

PLANTING MISTLETOE

Let the old tree be the gold tree;
Hand up the silver seed:
Let the hoary tree be the glory tree,
To shine out at need,
At mirth-time, at dearth-time,
Gold bough and milky bead.

For the root's failing and the shoot's failing;
Soon it will bloom no more.
The growth's arrested, the yaffle's nested
Deep in its hollow core:
Over the grasses thinly passes
The shade so dark before.

Save a few sprigs of the new twigs,
If any such you find:
Don't lose them, but use them,
Keeping a good kind
To be rooting and fruiting
When this is old and blind.

So the tragic tree is the magic tree,
Running the whole range
Of growing and blowing
And suffering change:
Then buying, by dying,
The wonderful and strange.

Ruth Pitter

ASPENS

All day and night, save winter, every weather,
Above the inn, the smithy and the shop,
The aspens at the cross-roads talk together
Of rain, until their last leaves fall from the top.

Out of the blacksmith's cavern comes the ringing
Of hammer, shoe and anvil; out of the inn
The clink, the hum, the roar, the random singing –
The sounds that for these fifty years have been.

The whisper of the aspens is not drowned,
And over lightless pane and footless road,
Empty as sky, with every other sound
Not ceasing, calls their ghosts from their abode,

A silent smithy, a silent inn, nor fails
In the bare moonlight or the thick-furred gloom,
In the tempest or the night of nightingales,
To turn the cross-roads to a ghostly room.

And it would be the same were no house near.
Over the sorts of weather, men, and times,
Aspens must shake their leaves and men may hear
But need not listen, more than to my rhymes.

Whatever wind blows, while they and I have leaves
We cannot other than an aspen be
That ceaselessly, unreasonably grieves,
Or so men think who like a different tree.

Edward Thomas

Flower-Lovers & Weed-Lovers

WEEDS

Some people are flower lovers.
I'm a weed lover.

Weeds don't need planting in well-drained soil;
They don't ask for fertilizer or bits of rag to scare away
    birds.
They come without invitation;
And they don't take the hint when you want them to go.
Weeds are nobody's guests:
More like squatters.

Coltsfoot laying claim to every new-dug clump of clay;
Pearlwort scraping up a living from a ha'porth of mortar;
Dandelions you daren't pick or you know what will happen;
Sour docks that make a first-rate poultice for nettle-stings;
And flat-foot plantain in the back street,
    gathering more dust than the dustmen.

Even the names are a folk-song:
Fat hen, rat's tail, cat's ear, old men's baccy and Stinking
    Billy
Ring a prettier chime for me than honeysuckle or jasmine,
And Sweet Cicely smells cleaner than Sweet William
    though she's barred from the garden.

And they have their uses, weeds.
Think of the old, worked-out mines –
Quarries and tunnels, earth scorched and scruffy,
    torn-up railways, splintered sleepers,
And a whole Sahara of grit and smother and cinders.

But go in summer and where is all the clutter?
For a new town has risen of a thousand towers,
Sparkling like granite, swaying like larches,
And every spiky belfry humming with a peal of bees.
Rosebay willowherb:
Only a weed!

Flowers are for wrapping in cellophane to present as a
    bouquet;
Flowers are for prize-arrangements in vases and silver
    tea-pots;
Flowers are for plaiting into funeral wreaths.
You can keep your flowers.
Give me weeds!

Norman Nicholson

TALL NETTLES

Tall nettles cover up, as they have done
These many springs, the rusty harrow, the plough
Long worn out, and the roller made of stone:
Only the elm butt tops the nettles now.

This corner of the farmyard I like most:
As well as any bloom upon a flower
I like the dust on the nettles, never lost
Except to prove the sweetness of a shower.

Edward Thomas

THISTLES

Thirty thirsty thistles
Thicketed and green
Growing in a grassy swamp
Purple-topped and lean
Prickily and thistley
Topped by tufts of thorns
Green mean little leaves on them
And tiny purple horns
Briary and brambley
A spikey, spiney bunch of them.
A troop of bright-red birds came by
And had a lovely lunch of them.

Karla Kuskin

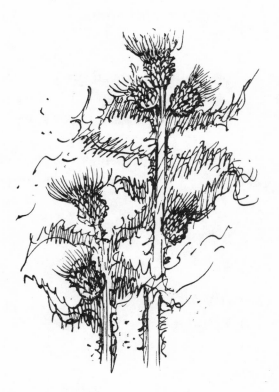

THISTLE

Thistle, blue bunch of daggers
rattling upon the wind,
saw-tooth that separates
the lips of grasses.

Your wound in childhood was
a savage shock of joy
that set the bees on fire
and the loud larks singing.

Your head enchanted then
smouldering among the flowers
filled the whole sky with smoke
and sparks of seed.

Now from your stabbing bloom's
nostalgic point of pain
ghosts of those summers rise
rustling across my eyes.

Seeding a magic thorn
to prick the memory,
to start in my icy flesh
fevers of long lost fields.

Laurie Lee

AN ABSENCE OF NETTLES

I like nettles, but I took
the cold scythe for your sake
To clean the way where you would walk
And make it possible
For your foreshadowed flowers.

An evening I worked there,
And another, longer; gripping
The ancient handles with a clumsy craft,
Swinging the rusty blade about my knees,
Crouched to listen to it.

The keen heads of nettles
Lopped without pity
Were raked and carried up
To a black-hearted bonfire;
The shaven earth was ready.

I pulled up such roots
As the hands can find,
And cast away pebbles;
Weeding and watering
My own grave.

But now – no flowers have come
To fit your shadows;
The earth will not accept
The seeds you sow. And who can care for
An absence of nettles, an ungrowing place?

Robert Nye

WHEN YOU WALK

When you walk in a field,
Look down
Lest you tramp
On a daisy's crown!

But in a city
Look always high,
And watch
The beautiful clouds go by!

James Stephens

DAISIES

Where innocent bright-eyed daisies are,
With blades of grass between,
Each daisy stands up like a star
Out of a sky of green.

Christina Rossetti

THE DAISIES

The rich and rare magnolia tree
    Has one white flower
Which blossoms in a single hour.
But in the common grass, oh, see!
    Daisies are found
In thousands near the whole year round.

Eleanor Farjeon

Girls who weave a daisy chain
Grow up pretty, never plain–

Anon

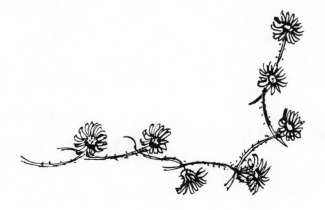

IF I SHOULD EVER BY CHANCE

If I should ever by chance grow rich
I'll buy Codham, Cockridden, and Childerditch,
Roses, Pyrgo, and Lapwater,
And let them all to my elder daughter.
The rent I shall ask of her will be only
Each year's first violets, white and lonely,
The first primroses and orchises–
She must find them before I do, that is.
But if she finds a blossom on furze
Without rent they shall all for ever be hers,
Whenever I am sufficiently rich:
Codham, Cockridden, and Childerditch,
Roses, Pyrgo and Lapwater,–
I shall give them all to my elder daughter.

Edward Thomas

CROCUSES

The sunrise tints the dew,
    The yellow crocuses are out –
And I must pick a few.

Anon

CAT AND CROCUSES

In the crocus-bed I saw her;
Like a queen enthroned she sat.
Yellow crocuses shone round her –
Royal, sun-illumined cat:

Orange eyes intensely lighted
By a vivid golden flame:
Fire of spring that burnt within her,
And in every flower the same.

World-surveying, world-contented,
Seated in her crocus-ring:
Cat and crocuses together
Basking in the fires of spring.

Eva Martin

SUMMER HEDGEROW

On a deep-shelved bank between field and lane
The hedgerows of June are in flower again,
And under a tangle of hawthorn grows
Foxglove, and speedwell, and the wild briar rose.

Red-robin, ragged-robin, stitchwort and clover
Come when the bluebell and primrose are over,
And near to the elm, at the ploughland's edge,
Stand Jack-in-the-Pulpit and Jack-by-the-Hedge.

Crowsfoot and cranesbill and bryony run
Through thorn-crossed shade into dappled sun;
And all those wildflowers the summer knows,
From meadowsweet to the sweet dog-rose,

Find their home here. Their roots take hold
In rich, moist earth and soft leaf-mould;
Their breath on the air of the Longest Day
Joins windblown grass and the scent of may.

Bindweed, woodbine, comfrey, sorrel,
Climb and twine in friendly quarrel,
And tenderly petal and leaf enclose
Foxglove, and speedwell, and the wild briar rose.

Clive Sansom

A CELEBRATION

You will know it, the ragwort,
Though not perhaps by name –
A yellow flower, full
Of mischief for the gardener.
A common weed, populous
As common people, and as apt
To make the best of an indifferent lot.
You will know its pertinacious ways,
Its bland possession of a tumbled soil,
And you will wonder why
I celebrate its impudence.

Well, I will tell you. There is a spot
In Cardiff where the Taff
Flows between grubby banks. The view
Is nonexistent. Concrete, bricks,
And traffic brash as pain.
Between the road and river runs
A row of rusty railings. And just here
The ragwort grows. A common weed.
But such a blaze of beauty that it blooms
Redemption on the urban blasphemy,
And justifies itself like Magdalene.

Herbert Williams

HEDGES

'Bread and cheese' grow wild in the green time,
Children laugh and pick it, and I make my rhyme
For mere pleasure of seeing that so subtle play
Of arms and various legs going every, any way.

And they turn and laugh for the unexpensiveness
Of country grocery and are pleased no less
Than hedge sparrows. Lessons will be easier taken,
For this gipsy chaffering, the hedge plucked and shaken.

Ivor Gurney

GREEN WINTER

A green winter, snow
in some ditches though stubbornly lingers,
very first primroses show,
grass pushes up new fingers,
window-panes carved still with frost triangles,
from branch to branch chaffinches flit,
here and there a catkin dangles,
and every blue and long-tailed tit
pretends to be a clown,
pecking at rind and nut,
viewing the garden upside down,
ice splinters now in each water-butt.

Then suddenly overnight
The golden surprise of one aconite.

Leonard Clark

Green the young herbs
In the fields of snow,
Green, O, how green!

after the Japanese of Raizan

I DIDN'T WANT ANYTHING NEW

But I didn't want anything new,
Only primroses growing where they always grew,
No, I didn't want anything new,

And I didn't want anything grand,
Only curlews calling over the tufted land,
No, I didn't want anything grand.

I only wanted to go
To the fields to see things grow,
And to wander to and fro –

Margaret Cropper

THE PRIMROSES

Ask me why I send you here
This sweet Infanta of the year?
Ask me why I send to you
This primose, thus bepearl'd with dew?
I will whisper to your ears:–
The sweets of love are mix'd with tears.

Ask me why this flower does show
So yellow-green, and sickly too?
Ask me why the stalk is weak
And bending (yet it doth not break)?
I will answer:– These discover
What fainting hopes are in a lover.

Robert Herrick

THE NATURE LESSON

The teacher has the flowers on her desk,
Then goes round, giving one to each of us.
We are going to study the primrose –
To find out all about it. It has five petals,
Notice the little dent in each, making it heart-shaped
And a pale green calyx (And O! the hairy stem!).
Now, in the middle of the flower
There may be a little knob – that is the pistil –
Or perhaps your flower may show the bunch of stamens.
        We look at our flowers
To find out which kind we have got.

Now we are going to look inside,
So pull your petals off, one by one.
        But wait . . .
If I pull my flower to pieces it will stop
Being a primrose. It will be just bits
Strewn on my desk. I can't pull it to pieces.
What does it matter what goes on inside?
I won't find out by pulling it to pieces,
Because it will not be a primrose any more,
And the bits will not mean anything at all.
A primrose is a primrose, not just bits.

It lies there, a five-petalled primrose,
A whole primrose, a living primrose.
To find out what is inside I make it dead,
And then it will not be a primrose.
                    You can't find out
What goes on inside a living flower that way.
The teacher talks, fingers rustle . . .
I will look over my neighbour's flower
And leave my primrose whole. But if the teacher comes
And tells me singly to pull my flower to pieces
Then I will do as I am told. The teacher comes,
Passes my neighbour on her gangway side,
Does not see my primrose is still whole,
Goes by, not noticing; nobody notices.

My flower remains a primrose, that they all
Want to find out about by pulling to pieces.
I am alone: all the world is alone
In the flower left breathing on my desk.

Marjorie Baldwin

ANN'S FLOWERS

Ann with hot fingers grasped her flowers
   A long half-day.
'See, they are withering, Ann; you'd best
   Throw them away.'

Yet still through lane and by-way on
   And on she trailed,
Till scent of flowers was one with warmth
   Of hand that held.

But when she knew that water now
   Would never bring
Freshness, she found a bank, with moss
   For covering;

There, lulled by reeds of grass and cooled
   By shade of tree,
A bed she made, in which they could
   Die quietly.

John Walsh

TO GEORGE PULLING BUDS

Don't pull that bud, it yet may grow
   As fine a flower as this;
Had this been pulled a month ago,
   We should its beauties miss.
You are yourself a bud, my blooming boy,
Weigh well the consequence, ere you destroy,
Lest for a present paltry sport, you kill a future joy.

Adelaide O'Keeffe

DANDELION

This is time's
(one o'clock, two o'clock)
golden head
wet the bed

flower;
forever turning its
(four o'clock, five o'clock)
face

to follow the sun.
But it's time that sets the
(seven o'clock, eight o'clock)
grey hairs growing

and will scythe off its
(eleven o'clock, twelve o'clock)
limp and wrinkled
ugly bald skull.

Neil Curry

THE FIRST DANDELION

Simple and fresh and fair from winter's close emerging,
As if no artifice of fashion, business, politics, had ever been,
Forth from its sunny nook of shelter'd grass – innocent,
   golden, calm as the dawn,
The spring's first dandelion shows its trustful face.

Walt Whitman

FLOATING DANDELION SEED

Wonderful wandering sky child
   seeking one piece of
      fertile soil

Alas, you don't find that
   in a railway station buffet
      so, you die.

But then, given time, a railway station
   buffet would kill us all.

Spike Milligan

KNOWING WHERE TO LOOK

Spongey green, mosses froth
on concrete; and what's this glued
into a crack in the pavement? a dandelion!
here, tough as boots, is dusty plantain;
while pimpling the tarmac, breaking through its black,
is horsetail poking green spikes.

See, in the gutter that old crust
of bread the sparrows missed
is alive with mould; and halfway up this wall
some wizard's thrown green stardust
to make the lichens grow.

But what about these acrobats?
the nerve of that double-jointed groundsel
teetering on the window ledge!
And him, five storeys up,
with his firework display of purple flowers,
him with that grand circus name
of rosebay willow herb . . .
do you think he's going to take off,
do you think he'll jump?

Matt Simpson

FLOWER IN THE CRANNIED WALL

Flower in the crannied wall,
I pluck you out of the crannies,
I hold you here, root and all, in my hand,
Little flower – but if I could understand
What you are, root and all, and all in all,
I should know what God and man is.

Alfred, Lord Tennyson

THE WILD FLOWER'S SONG

As I wander'd the forest,
The green leaves among,
I heard a Wild Flower
Singing a song.

'I slept in the earth
In the silent night,
I murmur'd my fears
And I felt delight.

'In the morning I went,
As rosy as morn,
To seek for new joy;
But I met with scorn.'

William Blake

WILD FLOWERS

'Of what are you afraid, my child?'
    inquired the kindly teacher.
'Oh, sir! the flowers, they are wild,'
    replied the timid creature.

Peter Newell

TO DAFFODILS

Fair Daffodils, we weep to see
    You haste away so soon:
As yet the early-rising Sun
    Has not attained his Noon.
      Stay, stay,
Until the hasting day
      Has run
    But to the Even-song;
And, having prayed together, we
    Will go with you along.

We have short time to stay, as you,
    We have as short a Spring;
As quick a growth to meet Decay,
    As you, or any thing.
      We die,
    As your hours do, and dry
    Away,
    Like to the Summer's rain;
Or as the pearls of Morning's dew
    Ne'er to be found again.

Robert Herrick

I WANDER'D LONELY AS A CLOUD

I wander'd lonely as a cloud
   That floats on high o'er vales and hills,
When all at once I saw a crowd,
   A host, of golden daffodils;
Beside the lake, beneath the trees,
Fluttering and dancing in the breeze.

Continuous as the stars that shine
   And twinkle on the Milky Way,
They stretch'd in never-ending line
   Along the margin of a bay:
Ten thousand saw I at a glance,
Tossing their heads in sprightly dance.

The waves beside them danced, but they
   Out-did the sparkling waves in glee:
A poet could not but be gay,
   In such a jocund company:
I gazed – and gazed – but little thought
What wealth the show to me had brought:

For oft, when on my couch I lie
   In vacant or in pensive mood,
They flash upon that inward eye
   Which is the bliss of solitude;
And then my heart with pleasure fills,
And dances with the daffodils.

William Wordsworth

THE POEM I'D LIKE TO WRITE

I'd like to write a poem about daffodils.
I'd like to say
How beautiful they look on a March day,
Their green stems rising
Into those large, incredibly surprising
Trumpets of pure gold;
And how, after frost and cold,
They bring
Such colour and such warmth to everything,
They shake us into Spring.

I'd like to write it, but I know
That Wordsworth wrote it long ago.

Clive Sansom

I LOVE . . .

I love the English country scene
But sometimes think there's too much Hooker's green,
Especially in August, when the flowers that might have lent a
Lightness, don't; being gamboge or magenta.

Stevie Smith

from GRANTCHESTER

Just now the lilac is in bloom,
All before my little room;
And in my flower-beds, I think,
Smile the carnation and the pink;
And down the borders, well I know,
The poppy and the pansy blow . . .
Oh! there the chestnuts, summer through,
Beside the river make for you
A tunnel of green gloom, and sleep
Deeply above; and green and deep
The stream mysterious glides beneath,
Green as a dream and deep as death.

Rupert Brooke

MADONNA LILY

O lovely lily clean
O lily springing green,
O lily bursting white. . .

John Masefield

THOSE LATIN NAMES

It was a simple country child
Who took me by the hand:
Why English flowers had Latin names
She couldn't understand.
Those funny, friendly English flowers,
That bloom from year to year –
She asked me if I would explain,
And so I said to her:

ERANTHIS is an aconite
As everybody knows,
And HELLEBORUS NIGER is
Our friend the Christmas rose.
GALANTHUS is a snowdrop,
MATTHIOLA is a stock,
And CARDAMINE the meadow flower
Which *you* call lady's smock.
MUSCARI is grape hyacinth,
DIANTHUS is a pink –
And that's as much as one small head
Can carry, I should think.

She listened, very patiently;
Then turned, when I had done,
To where a fine FORSYTHIA
Was smiling in the sun.

Said she: 'I *love* this yellow stuff.'
And that, somehow, seemed praise enough.

Reginald Arkell

TO ANY GARDEN

Garden, grow,
  In clump and row,
Golden trumpet, branch of snow,
Bell of blue and drop of white,
Swelling with your fill of light.

Garden, show your shades of green,
Spires of green, and blades of green,
Crinkled leaves upon whose bed
Little yellow stars are spread.

Garden, grow,
  Quick and slow,
Some surprise each morning show;
Lovely as your blue and gold,
Are the surprises you withhold.

Eleanor Farjeon

from INVERSNAID

What would the world be, once bereft
Of wet and wildness? Let them be left,
O let them be left, wildness and wet,
Long live the weeds and the wilderness yet.

Gerald Manley Hopkins

So They Are Felled

TREE

For eighty years he stood in the strong sun,
Gathering its power within him, storing its warmth
In bole and branch: its life was in his wood.
Then the tree died. Men came and lopped his limbs
And sliced his trunk into a hundred logs.
His strength has gone. But the stored heat is there:
And now, released in flame, it lives again
And pours across the room like winter sunlight.

Clive Sansom

from TREES

So they are felled . . . They change, they come,
Lingering their period of decay
In transitory forms . . .

And some, some trees, before they die,
Carved and moulded small,
Suddenly begin,
Oh, what a wild and windy woodland call
Out of the lips of the violin!

So trees are felled . . .

Harold Munro

FELLED TREES

Nobody has come to burn them,
Long green grass grows up between them,
Up between white boughs that lie
Dead and empty, dry,
That once were full of leaves and sky.

Ruth Dallas

BINSEY POPLARS

felled 1879

My aspens dear, whose airy cages quelled,
Quelled or quenched in leaves the leaping sun,
All felled, felled, are all felled;
    Of a fresh and following folded rank
        Not spared, not one
        That dandled a sandalled
      Shadow that swam or sank
On meadow and river and wind-wandering weed-winding bank.

O if we but knew what we do
      When we delve or hew –
    Hack and rack the growing green!
     Since country is so tender
    To touch, her being só slender,
    That, like this sleek and seeing ball
    But a prick will make no eye at all,
    Where we, even where we mean
      To mend her we end her,
    When we hew or delve:
After-comers cannot guess the beauty been.
  Ten or twelve, only ten or twelve
    Strokes of havoc únselve
     The sweet especial scene,
    Rural scene, a rural scene,
    Sweet especial rural scene.

Gerard Manley Hopkins

THE CHERRY STUMP

Years ago friends had a cherry tree,
big and dark in their front garden.
For one week in each year it flashed white
and for the rest did nothing
but breed dark in through the window.

It was badly planted, too close.
Its dirty bark scratted the guests' clothes,
its twigs brushed the gatepost.

They cut the tree down and the small bare
garden was bright, the windows were oblong,
not shifting lozenges beating back green.

They left a sudden stump and a frill of sawdust.
They had no choice but to poison the stump:
the tree would grow back on them, it must
rise up somehow, throwing out suckers.
Its life would snake up.

A big dark cherry like that, shaking itself –
it's not enough that you cut it to earth.
It has to be tracked through the soil by its roots
and where it is found, smoked out.

Helen Dunmore

THROWING A TREE

The two executioners stalk along over the knolls,
Bearing two axes with heavy heads shining and wide,
And a long limp two-handled saw toothed for cutting great boles,
And so they approach the proud tree that bears the death-mark on its
     side.

Jackets doffed they swing axes and chop away just above ground,
And the chips fly about and lie white on the moss and fallen
     leaves;
Till a broad deep gash in the bark is hewn all the way round,
And one of them tries to hook upward a rope, which at last he
     achieves.

The saw then begins, till the top of the tall giant shivers:
The shivers are seen to grow greater each cut than before:
They edge out the saw, tug the rope; but the tree only quivers,
And kneeling and sawing again, they step back to try pulling once
     more.

Then, lastly, the living mast sways, further sways: with a shout
Job and Ike rush aside. Reached the end of its long staying
     powers
The tree crashes downward: it shakes all its neighbours
     throughout,
And two hundred years' steady growth has been ended in less than two
     hours.

Thomas Hardy

TEN TALL OAKTREES

Ten tall oaktrees
Standing in a line,
'Warships,' cried King Henry,
Then there were nine.

Nine tall oaktrees
Growing strong and straight,
'Charcoal,' breathed the furnace,
Then there were eight.

Eight tall oaktrees,
Reaching towards heaven,
'Sizzle,' spoke the lightning,
Then there were seven.

Seven tall oaktrees,
Branches, leaves and sticks,
'Firewood,' smiled the merchant,
Then there were six.

Six tall oaktrees
Glad to be alive,
'Barrels,' boomed the brewery,
Then there were five.

Five tall oaktrees,
Suddenly a roar,
'Gangway,' screamed the west wind,
Then there were four.

Four tall oaktrees
Sighing like the sea,
'Floorboards,' beamed the builder,
Then there were three.

Three tall oaktrees
Groaning as trees do,
'Unsafe,' claimed the council,
Then there were two.

Two tall oaktrees
Spreading in the sun,
'Progress,' snarled the by-pass,
Then there was one.

One tall oaktree
Wishing it could run,
'Nuisance,' grumped the farmer,
Then there were none.

No tall oaktrees,
Search the fields in vain,
Only empty skylines
And the cold grey rain.

Richard Edwards

THE LURCHER

Forth goes the woodman, leaving unconcerned
The cheerful haunts of men to wield the axe
And drive the wedge in yonder forest drear,
From morn to eve his solitary task.
Shaggy and lean and shrewd, with pointed ears
And tail cropped short, half-lurcher and half-cur,
His dog attends him. Close behind his heel
Now creeps he slow, and now with many a frisk
Wide scampering, snatches up the drifted snow
With ivory teeth, or ploughs it with his snout;
Then shakes his powder'd coat, and barks for joy.

William Cowper

There was a young man from Brazil
Who cut down the trees on a hill.
It rained all one day
And the soil washed away
So life on the hill is now nil.

Colin Nicholls

VELLEN O'THE TREE

Aye, the girt elem tree out in little hwome groun'
Wer a-stannèn this mornèn, an' now's a-cut down.
Aye, the girt elem tree, so big roun' an' so high,
Where the mowers did goo to their drink, an' did lie
In the sheäde ov his head, when the zun at his heighth
Had a-ɖrove em vrom mowèn, wi' het an' wi' drîth,
Where the haÿ-meäkers put all their picks an' their reäkes,
An' did squot down to snabble their cheese an' their ceäkes,
An' did vill vrom their flaggons their cups wi' their eäle,
An' did meäke theirzelves merry wi' joke an' wi' teäle.

Ees, we took up a rwope an' we tied en all round
At the top o'n, wi' woone end a-hangèn to ground,
An' we cut, near the ground, his girt stem a' most drough,
An' we bent the wold head o'n wi' woone tug or two;
An' he swaÿ'd all his limbs, an' he nodded his head,
Till he vell away down like a pillar o'lead:
An' as we did run vrom en, there, clwose at our backs,
Oh! his boughs come to groun' wi' sich whizzes an' cracks;
An' his top wer so lofty that, now he is down,
The stem o'n do reach a'most over the groun'.
Zoo the girt elem tree out in little hwome groun'
Wer a-stannèn this mornèn, an' now's a-cut down.

William Barnes

THE AXE IN THE WOOD

I stopped to watch a man strike at the trunk
Of a tree grown strong through many centuries.
His quick axe, sharp and glittering, struck deep,
And yellow chips went spinning in the air –
And I remember how I liked the sight
Of poise and rhythm as the bright axe swung.
A man who fells a tree makes people watch,
For glory seems to crowd upon the axe.

I know the answers to the chance reproach:
How old the tree was, and how dangerous,
How it might fall, how timber in a stack
Had more good in it than a growing tree –
But I saw death cut down a thousand men
In that tall lovely legacy of wood.

Clifford Dyment

FIREWOOD

Sad handfuls of green air
Hang in the gloom. The sun
Nails tatters of foxfur
On the bark of larch and fir.

I find a tree poleaxed
By a hammerhead of wind –
Its roots a miser's fist;
Its slender branches crushed.

Death's scavenger, I lop
Them off. To the sawing-horse
I drag the dismembered corpse.
I saw the sunlight up.

– As though I have released
What was still imprisoned there,
The air is filled with scent,
The tree gives up its ghost.

Norman MacCaig

The tree casts its shade upon all,
  even upon the woodcutter.

Hindustani proverb

GOLIATH

They chop down 100ft trees
To make chairs
I bought one
I am six-foot one inch.
When I sit in the chair
I'm four foot two.
Did they really chop down a 100ft tree
To make me look shorter?

Spike Milligan

THE GREEN WOOD

Hit is no need eek for to axe
Wher there were many grenė grevis,
Or thikke of trees, so ful of levės;
And every tree stood by him-selve,
Fro other wel ten feet or twelve.
So gretė trees, so huge of strengthe,
Of fourty, or fifty fadmė lengthe,
Clene withoutė bough or stikke
With croppės brode and eek as thikke, –
They werė not an ynche a-sonder, –
That hit was shadwė over al under;
And many an hert and many an hynde
Was bothe before me and be-hynde.
　Of founės, sourės, bukkės, doės,
Was ful the wode; and many roės,
And many squirrelės, that sete
Ful heigh upon the trees and ete,
And in hir manėr madė festės.

Geoffrey Chaucer

THE TIRED TREE

In the soft earth the tips
　　Already show:
Green bulbs and spears and slips,
　　Promising oh
Such yellow daffodils,
　　Tulips so bright,
Snowdrops with double frills
　　Of green and white,
Crocus of mauve and gold,
　　And scylla blue,
Unfolding as of old,
　　And always new.
And pushed aside, forgot,
　　A tiny tree
In its December pot
　　Still here I see.
Its needles dusty are,
　　Its silver chain
And tarnished tinsel star
　　Past use again.
How tawdry you appear,
　　Small tree, to-day,
While knob and spire and spear
　　Grow green and gay;
Yet children who, for glee
　　Of flowers, cry 'Oh!'
Cried 'Oh!' at you, tired tree,
　　A month ago.
Come, I'll undress you now,
　　Your hour is dead;

I will unwind each bough
   Of silver thread,
For knob and spear and spire
   Shine in the sun,
And you must to my fire –
   The party's done.

Eleanor Farjeon

THE TREES

That summer along the M4
from London west to Bristol
every elm was dying or already dead.
Chain-saws smoked and yowled all day,
calling to each other across deserted fields.

The grand avenues of Wiltshire
paraded naked in July,
their branches bleached to finger bones
like the hands that tamped the soil round their soft roots.
Pyres spat and crackled on for weeks.

Why the Cornish elms survived so long is still uncertain;
like the people, they are a different strain.
Southwesterly gales slowed the progress of the pest;
skyline trees reprieved by the wind that crippled them.

And trees shadowing creekland coombes
like ancient architecture were spared
at first, the pestilence hesitating,
stung by salt in the air.

Most beautiful was the lane down to the bulb-field,
A south aisle pillared with elms
feathering their fan vaulting
in Perpendicular style.

Sunlight flickered
with stained glass intricacy
through the leaded tracery
of twigs and leaves.

Beneath, the holy air
was always cool and still,
the smells damp, fungal.
Foxgloves stood chorister tall.

Julian May

TO A TELEGRAPH POLE

You should be done with blossoming by now.
Yet here are leaves closer than any bough
That welcome ivy. True, you were a tree
And stood with others in a marching line,
Less regular than this, of spruce and pine,
And boasted branches rather than a trunk.
This is your final winter, all arms shrunk
To one cross-bar bearing haphazardly
Four rusty strands. You cannot hope to feel
The electric sap run through those veins of steel.
The birds know this; the birds have hoodwinked you,
Crowding about you as they used to do.
The rainy robins huddled on your wire
And those black birds with shoulders dipped in fire
Have made you dream these vines; these tendrils are
A last despair in green, familiar
To derelicts of earth as well as sea.
Do not believe them, there is mockery
In their cool little jets of song. They know
What everyone but you learned long ago:
The stream of stories humming through your head
Is not your own. You dream. But you are dead.

Louis Untermeyer

MY OWN TRUE FAMILY

Once I crept in an oakwood – I was looking for
   a stag.
I met an old woman there – all knobbly stick
   and rag.
She said: 'I have your secret here inside my
   little bag.'

Then she began to cackle and I began to quake.
She opened up her little bag and I came twice
   awake –
Surrounded by a staring tribe and me tied to a
   stake.

They said: 'We are the oak-trees and your own
   true family.
We are chopped down, we are torn up, you do
   not blink an eye.
Unless you make a promise now – now you are
   going to die.

Whenever you see an oak-tree felled, swear now
   you will plant two.
Unless you swear, the black oak bark will
   wrinkle over you
And root you among the oaks where you were
   born but never grew.'

This was my dream beneath the boughs, the
    dream that altered me.
When I came out of the oakwood, back to
    human company,
My walk was the walk of a human child, but my
    heart was a tree.

Ted Hughes

DOMUS CAEDET ARBOREM

Ever since the great planes were murdered at the end of the
        gardens,
The city, to me, at night has the look of a Spirit brooding
        crime;
As if the dark houses watching the trees from dark windows
        Were simply biding their time.

Charlotte Mew

Goodbye to Hedges

PROGRESS

The country is getting so terribly neat,
I think I should faint if I happened to meet
   A man with a load of hay:
You *never* see ricks in a rickyard now;
They turn on a switch when they milk a cow;
   They'll get it so smart, one day,
There won't be a spot
In the world we've got
   For a bird or a boy to play.

Reginald Arkell

QUESTION

As asphalt and concrete
Replace bushes and trees,
As highways and buildings
Replace marshes and woods,
What will replace
The song of the birds?

Tony Chen

127

CYNDDYLAN ON A TRACTOR

Ah, you should see Cynddylan on a tractor.
Gone the old look that yoked him to the soil;
He's a new man now, part of the machine,
His nerves of metal and his blood oil.
The clutch curses, but the gears obey
His least bidding, and lo, he's away
Out of the farmyard, scattering hens.
Riding to work now as a great man should,
He is the knight at arms breaking the fields'
Mirror of silence, emptying the wood
Of foxes and squirrels and bright jays.
The sun comes over the tall trees
Kindling all the hedges, but not for him
Who runs his engine on a different fuel.
And all the birds are singing, bills wide in vain,
As Cynddylan passes proudly up the lane.

R. S. Thomas

IF FLOWERS WANT TO GROW

If flowers want to grow
right out of concrete sidewalk cracks
I'm going to bend down to smell them

David Ignatow

BELEAGUERED CITIES

Build your houses, build your houses, build your towns,
Fell the woodland, to a gutter turn the brook,
Pave the meadows, pave the meadows, pave the downs,
   Plant your bricks and mortar where the grasses shook,
   The wind-swept grasses shook.
Build, build your Babels black against the sky –
But mark yon small green blade, your stones between,
   The single spy
Of that uncounted host you have outcast;
For with their tiny pennons waving green
   They shall storm your streets at last.

Build your houses, build your houses, build your slums,
   Drive your drains where once the rabbits used to lurk,
Let there be no song there save the wind that hums
   Through the idle wires while dumb men tramp to work,
   Tramp to their idle work.
Silent the siege; none notes it; yet one day
Men from your walls shall watch the woods once more
   Close round their prey.
Build, build the ramparts of your giant-town;
Yet they shall crumble to the dust before
   The battering thistle-down.

F.L. Lucas

SONG

A willow herb stunted and small
Ho hey wither away
Grew from a crack in a factory wall
Where nothing else would grow at all
By the bus-stop forty-nine O

There had never been a flower in that street
Ho hey wither away
Nothing but wheels and trampling feet
And the smell of tripe and butcher's meat
By the bus-stop forty-nine O

The willow herb put out frail shoots
Ho hey wither away
The purple buds the feathery fruits
Fell beneath a line of boots
At the bus-stop forty-nine O

Boots and buses have no pity
Ho hey wither away
A willow herb however pretty
Can have no future in a city
By the bus-stop forty-nine O

Olive Dehn

NOWHERE TO PLAY

Nowhere to play;
Backstreets and alleyways,
Car-parks and main roads;
Noise, dirt and danger all day.
Same old smells;
Exhaust, cars,
People, rubbish,
No smells of earth after rain.
Same old noises;
Rush of traffic,
Cops on their way;
'Where's the ice-cream man today?'

No new sensations;
Same hard pavements,
No mud to explore.
No pebbles, no pieces of wood to arrange.
Big buildings,
Big buses, big people;
No bee on a buttercup,
No ants on their way.
No green grass, just concrete,
No thrush song, just sirens.
Seasons passing unnoticed;
Nowhere to play –
'What's on telly today?'

Nicola Tyson

THE PARK

In the middle of the city
Is an open space called a Park;
It is difficult for us to do what we like there
Even after dark.

In the middle of the Park there is a statue,
A huge man made of stone;
We are not allowed to climb his legs or scribble on
   his trousers,
He has to be left alone.

In the middle of the grass there is some water
Surrounded by an asphalt path;
We are forbidden to fish or throw stones into it
Or swim or take a bath.

In the middle of the water is an island
Full of mysterious things,
But none of us has ever set foot upon it
Because none of us has wings.

Olive Dehn

HOUSING SCHEME

All summer through
The field drank showers of larksong;
Offering in return
The hospitality of grasses,
And flowers kneedeep.

Over those wide acres
Trooped the plovers,
Mourning and lamenting as evening fell.
From the hedgerows
Where the foam of meadowsweet broke,
The rabbits and mice
Peeped out, and boldly sat in the sun.

But when the oaks were bronzing,
Steamrollers and brickcarts
Broke through the hedges.
The white-haired grasses, and the seedpods
Disappeared into the mud,
And the larks were silent, the plovers gone.

Then over the newlaid roads
And the open trenches of drains,
Rose a hoarding to face the highway,
'Build your house in the country'.

Richard Church

SHADES OF GREEN

An eyesore – just a useless piece of land
before this new development was planned.

Some locals came for so-called recreation
– wasted on the younger generation.

Now supervised activities all day
attract a nicer class prepared to pay

for them. Our garage will promote Lead Free,
the supermarket stocks no C.F.C.

All food containers are degradable,
we place No Smoking signs on every table.

Values here are represented in
well tended borders of abundant green.

Pat Amick

SONG OF THE OPEN ROAD

I think that I shall never see
A billboard lovely as a tree.
Perhaps, unless the billboards fall,
I'll never see a tree at all.

Ogden Nash

COOL MEDIUM

In fifty-three the children up our road
Got television and disappeared indoors
After school, instead of coming out
To toast crusts over stick fires in the hedgerow
Or fill the first-starred, batwinged dusks of autumn
With clamour of wild games. I sulked around

The silent woods, refused their invitations,
And hated ever since those moon-grey flickers
From a dead planet. Now, at night, I still
Walk past curtained windows, knowing each
Conceals that strange communion. Is life
Something to be given up for that?

Amused, superior, grown-up faces smile:
The awkward child stalks in the woodland still,
Keeping the ward of long-abandoned places,
As if one day the others might come back,
Stubborn in an antique heresy,
With trees and winter stars for company.

David Sutton

WHY DID THEY KNOCK DOWN THE TREES, DADDY?

It's a question of standards, boy; standards of living.
It's cars, you see, that give us a high level of living –
help, so to speak, to set the thing in motion –
and if they also give us a high level of dying
that's incidental, a fringe benefit, a lottery
likely to hand out unexpected promotion.

Without cars, let's face it, a nation is under-developed,
And these days it's bad to be under-developed in anything at all –
Bust, thighs, muscles, sex or ego,
it's a competitive world, son.

The trees? Oh, well they have to go
on the advice of Big Brother
so that the cars can have a better chance
of hitting one another.

Colin Thiele

INEXPENSIVE PROGRESS

Encase your legs in nylons,
Bestride your hills with pylons
   O age without a soul;
Away with gentle willows
And all the elmy billows
   That through your valleys roll.

Let's say good-bye to hedges
And roads with grassy edges
   And winding country lanes;
Let all things travel faster
Where motor-car is master
   Till only Speed remains.

Destroy the ancient inn-signs
But strew the roads with tin signs
   'Keep Left', 'M4', 'Keep Out!'
Command, instruction, warning,
Repetitive adorning
   The rockeried roundabout;

For every raw obscenity
Must have its small 'amenity',
   Its patch of shaven green,
And hoardings look a wonder
In banks of floribunda
   With floodlights in between.

Leave no old village standing
Which could provide a landing
    For aeroplanes to roar,
But spare such cheap defacements
As huts with shattered casements
    Unlived-in since the war.

Let no provincial High Street
Which might be your or my street
    Look as it used to do,
But let the chain stores place here
Their miles of black glass facia
    And traffic thunder through.

And if there is some scenery,
Some unpretentious greenery,
    Surviving anywhere,
It does not need protecting
For soon we'll be erecting
    A Power Station there.

When all our roads are lighted
By concrete monsters sited
    Like gallows overhead
Bathed in the yellow vomit
Each monster belches from it,
    We'll know that we are dead.

John Betjeman

In the Greening Time

CLOCK-A-CLAY

In the cowslip pips I lie,
Hidden from the buzzing fly,
While green grass beneath me lies,
Pearled with dew like fishes' eyes.
Here I lie, a clock-a-clay,
Waiting for the time of day.

While grassy forest quakes surprise,
And the wild wind sobs and sighs,
My gold home rocks as like to fall,
On its pillar green and tall:
When the pattering rain drives by
Clock-a-clay keeps warm and dry.

Day by day and night by night,
All the week I hide from sight;
In the cowslip pips I lie,
In rain and dew still warm and dry;
Day and night, and night and day,
Red, black-spotted clock-a-clay.

My home shakes in wind and showers,
Pale green pillar topped with flowers,
Bending at the wild wind's breath,
Till I touch the grass beneath;
Here I live, lone clock-a-clay,
Watching for the time of day.

John Clare

CATERPILLAR

He stands on the suckers under his tail,
stretches forward and puts down
his six legs. Then he brings up
the sucker under his tail, making
a beautiful loop.

That's his way of walking. He makes
a row of upside-down U's
along the rib of a leaf. He is as green
as it.

The ways of walking! – horse, camel,
snail, me, crab, rabbit –
all inventing a way of journeying
till they become like the green caterpillar
that now stands on his tail

on the very tip of the leaf and sways, sways
like a tiny charmed snake,
groping in empty space for a foothold
where none is, where there is no
foothold at all.

Norman MacCaig

CATERPILLAR GOING SOMEWHERE

Its green face looks as if
it were about to spit – pft.

It moves along a twig
by doing exercises, bend, stretch –

hard to imagine
a potbellied caterpillar.

It looks so active (hard to imagine it
in the lotus position)

and yet, and yet
it looks so melancholy.

Is it because it knows that
when it reaches a green leaf

its jaws will open sideways
instead of up and down? . . .

It's standing erect now – it turns
from side to side

like a retired sea-captain
scanning horizons.

Norman MacCaig

CATERPILLAR

A fuzzy fellow, without feet,
Yet doth exceeding run!
Of velvet, is his Countenance,
And his Complexion, dun!

Sometime, he dwelleth in the grass!
Sometime, upon a bough,
From which he doth descend in plush
Upon the Passer-by!

All this in summer.
But when winds alarm the Forest Folk,
He taketh *Damask* Residence –
And struts in sewing silk!

Then, finer than a Lady,
Emerges in the spring!
A Feather on each shoulder!
You'd scarce recognize him!

By Men, yclept Caterpillar!
By me! But who am I,
To tell the pretty secret
Of the Butterfly!

Emily Dickinson

BRAMBLE TALK

A caterpillar on a leaf
Said sadly to another –
'So many pretty butterflies . . .
I wonder which one's Mother.'

Richard Edwards

BEAUTY ETERNAL

Today I saw a butterfly,
    The first-born of the spring,
Sunning itself upon a bank –
    A lovely tawny thing.

I saw a dandelion, too,
    As golden as the sun;
And these will still be beautiful
    When all the wars are done.

Teresa Hooley

THE SAFFRON BUTTERFLY

Out of its dark cocoon,
Like a blossom breaking earth
A saffron-wingéd butterfly
Came to its April birth,
Fluttered by banks of primroses:
I could not tell, not I,
If yellow butterflies starred the hedge,
Or a flower flew in the sky.

Teresa Hooley

THE EXAMPLE

Here's an example from
    A Butterfly;
That on a rough, hard rock
    Happy can lie;
Friendless and all alone
On this unsweetened stone.

Now let my bed be hard,
    No care take I;
I'll make my joy like this
    Small Butterfly;
Whose happy heart has power
To make a stone a flower.

W.H. Davies

BUTTERFLIES

Let's go to the green hills, you butterflies;
    tiger butterflies, you are also welcome.
When it gets dark, we will sleep among flowers;
    Or on leaves if the flowers bid us no welcome.

Anon

ON THE GRASSHOPPER AND CRICKET

The poetry of earth is never dead:
    When all the birds are faint with the hot sun,
    And hide in cooling trees, a voice will run
From hedge to hedge about the new-mown mead;
That is the Grasshopper's – he takes the lead
    In summer luxury, – he has never done
    With his delights; for when tired out with fun
He rests at ease beneath some pleasant weed.
The poetry of earth is ceasing never:
    On a lone winter evening, when the frost
    Has wrought a silence, from the stove there shrills
The Cricket's song, in warmth increasing ever,
    And seems to one in drowsiness half lost,
    The Grasshopper's among some grassy hills.

John Keats

MAGIC

Through my lens, this greenfly on a rose-leaf
Becomes in an eye-wink a terrifying monster
Crouching upon the dark-green leathery surface:
Beside him shines a bright round bubble of dew.
How odd, how fearful the world must look to him
As he stares through *his* lens! He sees my face
(Forehead and curving nose and one huge eye
Looming down coldly at him, prying and peering);
My cat, green-tiger-striped with shadow; and that lizard,
A sliding pterodactyl, as it passes
Through the tall, tangled forest of the grasses.

Clive Sansom

Greenfly, it's difficult to see
why God, who made the rose, made thee?

A.P. Herbert

LIVING

The fire in leaf and grass
so green it seems
each summer the last summer.

The wind blowing, the leaves
shivering in the sun,
each day the last day.

A red salamander
so cold and so
easy to catch, dreamily

moves his delicate feet
and long tail. I hold
my hand open for him to go.

Each minute the last minute.

Denise Levertov

THE LIZARD

If on any warm day when you ramble around
Among moss and dead leaves, you should happen to see
A quick trembling thing dart and hide on the ground,
And you search in the leaves, you would uncover me.

Thomas Hardy

THE FROGS' HISTORY

You caught and carried us, pleased with yourselves.
We were only blobs of black in jars.

You knew what we'd become, were glad to wait.
How hectically we swam in that glass cage!

And there was never hope of an escape.
You put us on a shelf with more care than

You generally move. We were a hope,
A something-to-look-forward-to, a change.

Almost a conjuring trick. Some sleight of nature
Would, given time, change us to your possessions.

We would be green and glossy, wet to touch.
'Take them away,' squeamish grown-ups would

Call out. Not you. You longed to hold us in
Your dry palms with surprising gentleness

And with a sense of unexpected justice
Would let us go, wanted to see us leap

And watch our eyes which never seem to sleep,
Hear our hideous but lively croak.

We know as well as you we are a joke.

Elizabeth Jennings

FROG

The spotted frog
Sits quite still
On a wet stone;

He is green
With a luster
Of water on his skin;

His back is mossy
With spots, and green
Like moss on a stone;

His gold-circled eyes
Stare hard
Like bright metal rings;

When he leaps
He is like a stone
Thrown into the pond;

Water rings spread
After him, bright circles
Of green, circles of gold.

Valerie Worth

TOAD AND FROG

Speckle-black Toad and freckle-green Frog,
Hopping together from quag to bog;
From pool into puddle
Right on they huddle;
Through thick and through thin,
Without tail or fin;
Croakle goes first and *Quackle* goes after,
Plash in the flood
And plump in the mud,
With slippery heels
Vaulting over the eels,
And mouths to their middles split down
    with laughter!
  Hu! hu! hex!

George Darley

On a leaf, a leaf
    casts a swaying green shadow –
    and the tree-frog sings!

O. Mabson-Southard

THE RIVALS

I heard a bird at dawn
Singing sweetly on a tree,
That the dew was on the lawn,
And the wind was on the lea;
But I didn't listen to him,
For he didn't sing to me!

I didn't listen to him,
For he didn't sing to me
That the dew was on the lawn,
And the wind was on the lea!
I was singing at the time,
Just as prettily as he!

I was singing all the time,
Just as prettily as he,
About the dew upon the lawn,
And the wind upon the lea!
So I didn't listen to him,
As he sang upon a tree!

James Stephens

A GREEN CORNFIELD

The earth was green, the sky was blue:
   I saw and heard one sunny morn
A skylark hang between the two,
   A singing speck above the corn;

A stage below, in gay accord,
   White butterflies danced on the wing,
And still the singing skylark soared,
   And silent sank and soared to sing.

The cornfield stretched a tender green
   To right and left beside my walks;
I knew he had a nest unseen
   Somewhere among the million stalks.

And as I paused to hear his song
   While swift the sunny moments slid,
Perhaps his mate sat listening long,
   And listened longer than I did.

Christina Rossetti

THE KINGFISHER

It was the Rainbow gave thee birth,
  And left thee all her lovely hues;
And, as her mother's name was Tears,
  So runs it in thy blood to choose
For haunts the lonely pools, and keep
In company with trees that weep.

Go you and, with such glorious hues,
  Live with proud Peacocks in green parks;
On lawns as smooth as shining glass,
  Let every feather show its marks;
Get thee on boughs and clap thy wings
Before the windows of proud kings.

Nay, lovely Bird, thou art not vain;
  Thou hast no proud, ambitious mind;
I also love a quiet place
  That's green, away from all mankind;
A lonely pool, and let a tree
Sigh with her bosom over me.

W.H. Davies

SUMMER

Rushes in a watery place,
   And reeds in a hollow;
A soaring skylark in the sky,
   A darting swallow;
And where pale blossom used to hang
   Ripe fruit to follow.

Christina Rossetti

SLENDER-BILLED PARAKEET

The tree had so many leaves
it was toppling with treasure,
from so much green it blinked
and never closed its eyes.

That's no way to sleep.

But the fluttering foliage
went flying off green and alive,
each bud learned to fly,
and the tree was left naked
weeping in the winter rain.

Pablo Neruda

THE WOOD WARBLER, THE WILLOW WARBLER & THE CHIFFCHAFF

I thought the leaves had come to life;
It was the leaf-green birds.

I thought the green leaves
Had found their singing voice – the high sweet trill,
The tinkling chimes dying away,
The soft *zip-zap* of earliest spring.

John Heath-Stubbs

THE GREEN WOODPECKER

He is the green-plumed popinjay of our northern woods,
Lunatic laugher of spring, destroyer
Of the ants' citadel.
He is loved by the Thunder God, and the nymphs
Of the druid oak-groves.

John Heath-Stubbs

THE GREENFINCH

On a May morning,
In the greening time
I heard a greenfinch in a college garden
Set to his jargon in a leafy tree;
The long flat call-note, which will be repeated
Through all the hot and dusty days of summer,
Subsumed in a desultory twitter.
The lazy greenfinch, thick-set country cousin
Of the trim, suburban, caged canary –
Green, green, green he calls through the green leaves.

John Heath-Stubbs

THE GREENFINCH

A greenfinch to my garden came,
A sober bird of simple hue;
Stout, philosophic, almost tame,
And only greener than the yew.

At length he rose, with flame-like play,
A changeling: – I can see him still
One moment glance, then dart away
With greenish lights and daffodil.

M.M. Johnson

LETTER FROM A SCHOOL-BOY IN THE COUNTRY TO HIS MOTHER IN TOWN

Dear Mother,–   Now sweet spring is come;
I hear the busy insects hum,
The frogs at eve are daily peeping,
Who the long winter have been sleeping.
All things are waked to life together,
By these soft showers, and warm spring weather.
The birds, their curious nests are making –
Hair, moss, and wool I see them taking.
O who would think a little bird,
Who cannot speak a single word,
Could go to work so true and steady?
Their nests will very soon be ready
To put their pretty eggs so blue in,
Which thoughtless boys so like to ruin.
How can they, for the short-lived pleasure,
Spoil such a pretty, precious treasure?
The grass is here a brighter green,
Than ever I before have seen:
Thickly with dandelions dotted,
And our play-ground, too, is spotted
With its soft, round, bright yellow face;
Sure 'tis a beauty in its place.
Oh mother, if I could but stay,
I'd write to you of spring all day.
I have much to tell, when I return,
But now, my lessons I must learn;
The school-bell rings, the boys are gone,
Your loving son, dear mother,

JOHN

Anon

WRITTEN IN PRISON

I envy e'en the fly its gleams of joy.
In the green woods, from being but a boy
Among the vulgar and the lowly bred,
I envied e'en the hare her grassy bed.
Innured to strife and hardship from a child,
I traced with lonely step the desert wild,
Sigh'd o'er bird pleasures but no nest destroyed,
With pleasure felt the singing they enjoyed,
Saw nature smile on all and shed no tears.
A slave through ages though a child in years,
The mockery and scorn of those more old,
An Esop in the worlds extended fold,
The fly I envy, settling in the sun
On the green leaf and wish my goal was won.

John Clare

In the name of the bee
And of the butterfly
And of the breeze
Amen.

Emily Dickinson

Bird-World, Leaf-Life

CHILDREN AT PLAY

'And I shall be a tree,'
The child said to a playmate. He went on,
'You are the river I am growing near,'
And to a third he said, 'You are the boat
Which rows across my clear, fresh water.' So
The ring-leader decided and the game
Went on for days, for weeks. Sometimes a word

Was heard by parents who looked baffled. They
Had quite forgotten how imagination
Had worked with them once. Certainly some have
More intense ones but there can be few
Children who lack some small creative power
Which is how an imagination shows
Itself. But it grows dim. That boy who played

At trees and rivers grew up with no gift
For any art but he became adept
At science and computers. Now he has
Children who, in a year or two, will play
The kind of game he knew. Will he forget
Just how it felt or be quite otherwise,
Feel the cold shudder of a large regret?

Elizabeth Jennings

NEW HAMPSHIRE

Children's voices in the orchard
Between the blossom- and the fruit-time:
Golden head, crimson head,
Between the green tip and the root.
Black wing, brown wing, hover over;
Twenty years and the spring is over;
To-day grieves, to-morrow grieves,
Cover me over, light-in leaves;
Golden head, black wing,
Cling, swing,
Spring, sing,
Swing up into the apple-tree.

T.S. Eliot

EVERY TIME I CLIMB A TREE

Every time I climb a tree
Every time I climb a tree
Every time I climb a tree
I scrape a leg
Or skin a knee
And every time I climb a tree
I find some ants
Or dodge a bee
And get the ants
All over me

And every time I climb a tree
Where have you been?
They say to me
But don't they know that I am free
Every time I climb a tree?
I like it best
To spot a nest
That has an egg
Or maybe three

And then I skin
The other leg
But every time I climb a tree
I see a lot of things to see
Swallows rooftops and TV
And all the fields and farms there be
Every time I climb a tree
Though climbing may be good for ants
It isn't awfully good for pants
But still it's pretty good for me
Every time I climb a tree

David McCord

from THE OAK-TREE

The girt woak tree that's in the dell!
Ther's noo tree I da love so well;
Var in thik tree, when I wer young,
I of'en climb'd an' of'en zwung,
An' pick'd the green-rin'd yacors, shed
In wrestlèn storm-winds vrom his head.
An' down below's the cloty brook
Wher I did vish wi' line an' hook,
An' beät, in plâysome dips an' zwims,
The foamy stream wi' white-skinn'd lims.
An' there my mother nimbly shot
Her knittèn-needles, as she zot
At evemen down below the wide
Woak's head, wi' fāther at her zide.
An' I've a plây'd wi' many a buoy,
That's now a man an' gone awoy;
     Zoo I da like noo tree so well
     'S the girt woak tree that's in the dell.

William Barnes

DAMSON TREE

Bark scuffs my thighs
as I inch into shade,

fruit cool-hanging,
chandeliers in church.

The nest coracles
four blue eggs,

a note, in capitals,
'John, do not harm these'.

John Latham

WHO?

I'm sure it wasn't me who spoke
When I was shinning up the oak,
So who, as I climbed up that tree,
Said: 'Get those nasty feet off me!'

Richard Edwards

WHEN I WAS A BIRD

I climbed up the karaka tree
Into a nest all made of leaves
But soft as feathers
I made up a song that went on singing all by itself
And hadn't any words but got sad at the end.
There were daisies in the grass under the tree.
I said, just to try them:
'I'll bite off your heads and give them to my little children to eat.'
But they didn't believe I was a bird
They stayed quite open.
The sky was like a blue nest with white feathers
And the sun was the mother bird keeping it warm.
That's what my song said: though it hadn't any words.
Little Brother came up the path, wheeling his barrow
I made my dress into wings and kept very quiet
Then when he was quite near I said: 'sweet – sweet.'
For a moment he looked quite startled –
Then he said: 'Pooh, you're not a bird; I can see your legs.'
But the daisies didn't really matter
And Little Brother didn't really matter –
I felt *just* like a bird.

Katherine Mansfield

Annihilating all that's made
to a green thought in a green shade . . .

Andrew Marvell

GREEN

Green, green, leaf-green,
the horse in the high field
grazing his dream . . .
cool docks by the stream
to soothe the sting . . .
rain dusts the leaves clean,
the air tastes green.

The woods are green,
Eden-green;
from deep in the shade
the children scream;
their hair glints green,
their lips taste of earth –
they can't leave the green.

They will not come in,
even to tales of the green
frog-prince, the laughing
head of a knight, green,
of good Sir Gawain
and the lady, a sword
laid between.

The grass on the green
is stroked by the stream:
playful water, clear on green . . .
Babbling of it, I mean –
other words, like *you*, like *me*
annihilated in
this one syllable, green.

Brian Lee

CHILDHOOD

I see all, am all, all.
I leap along the line of the horizon hill,
I am a cloud in the high sky,
I trace the veins of intricate fern,
In the dark ivy wall the wren's world
Soft to bird breast nest of round eggs is mine,
Mine in the rowan-tree the blackbird's thought
Inviolate in leaves ensphered.
I am bird-world, leaf-life, I am wasp-world hung
Under low berry-branch of hidden thorn,
Friable paper-world humming with hate,
Moss-thought, rain-thought, stone still thought on the hill.

Never, never, never will I go home to be a child.

Kathleen Raine

For Those Born Later

EXPERIMENTAL TWIG

Experimental twig
  planted by a child
now waves before the window,
  tree-size, and wild.

While it's been so growing
  four years in the grass
my life's been withdrawing
  into small compass.

Neither in the balance
  weighing very much
– but one has gained in beauty,
  one has lost touch.

Molly Holden

SEEDS

The seeds I sowed –
For weeks unseen –
Have pushed up pygmy
Shoots of green;
So frail you'd think
The tiniest stone
Would never let
A glimpse be shown.
But no; a pebble
Near them lies,
At least a cherry-stone
In size,
Which that mere sprout
Has heaved away,
To bask in sunshine,
See the Day.

Walter de la Mare

A SPIKE OF GREEN

When I went out
The sun was hot,
It shone upon
My flower pot.

And there I saw
A spike of green
That no one else
Had ever seen!

On other days
The things I see
Are mostly old
Except for me.

But this green spike
So new and small
Had never yet
Been seen at all!

Barbara Baker

TRANSPLANTING

Watching hands transplanting,
Turning and tamping,
Lifting the young plants with two fingers,
Sifting in a palm-full of fresh loam,–
One swift movement,–
Then plumping in the bunched roots,
A single twist of the thumbs, a tamping and turning,
All in one,
Quick on the wooden bench,
A shaking down, while the stem stays straight,
Once, twice, and a faint third thump,–
Into the flat-box it goes,
Ready for the long days under the sloped glass:

The sun warming the fine loam,
The young horns winding and unwinding,
Creaking their thin spines,
The underleaves, the smallest buds
Breaking into nakedness,
The blossoms extending
Out into the sweet air,
The whole flower extending outward,
Stretching and reaching.

Theodore Roethke

THE POEM

It is only a little twig
With a green bud at the end;
But if you plant it,
And water it,
And set it where the sun will be above it,
It will grow into a tall bush
With many flowers,
And leaves which thrust hither and thither
Sparkling.
From its roots will come freshness,
And beneath it the grass-blades
Will bend and recover themselves,
And clash one upon another
In the blowing wind.

But if you take my twig
And throw it into a closet
With mousetraps and blunted tools,
It will shrivel and waste.
And, some day,
When you open the door,
You will think it an old twisted nail,
And sweep it into the dust bin
With other rubbish.

Amy Lowell

ACORN HAIKU

Just a green olive
In its own little egg-cup:
It can feed the sky.

Kit Wright

TO A CONKER

Glossy horse-chestnut
foal, if you do not today
fall on luck &
found a horse-
chestnut tree, tomorrow
will have you defeated,
meagre, matt-coated,
unsheltered, shrunk, bony-ribbed, and, perhaps,
tied to a string; – so
land on Good Luck; conquer!

Gerda Mayer

THE CONKER-TREE

Dog and foal
Sniff each other
Through the fence.
Each ready to retreat
If the meeting does not go well,
But kind speaks to kind
With cautious affection.

Pleased with himself
The dog picks up a conker
and brings it to me.
From the brown, shiny surface
A green shoot
Investigates the possibilities.

In time the tree has grown tall
And the dog has died,
The arch of his life complete.

But this year his tree has produced a flower.

David King

TREE-PLANTING

(for Julien)

Five-year-olds plant an oak,
press the roots firm, their gift.
Late-autumn cold chills, distracts
but they fight back
with cheers and hugs
down their conga-line.

They are making a pact
for all the trees of their lives –
chosen forests:
trees they will draw and colour,
fill with birds and flaring-golds
– that they will climb

stand under in the rain
and be hidden by,
that they will keep
to gird rainforests:
mantled, drenched in a lattice
of undergrowth and light.

Katherine Gallagher

He that plants trees loves others besides himself.

TRACEY'S TREE

Last year it was not there,
the sapling with purplish leaves
planted in our school grounds with care.
It's Tracey's tree, my friend who died,
and last year it was not there.

Tracey, the girl with long black hair
who, out playing one day, ran
across a main road for a dare.
The lorry struck her. Now a tree grows
and last year it was not there.

Through the classroom window I stare
and watch the sapling sway.
Soon its branches will stand bare.
It wears a forlorn and lonely look
and last year it was not there.

October's chill is in the air
and cold rain distorts my view.
I feel a sadness that's hard to bear.
The tree blurs, as if I've been crying,
and last year it was not there.

Wes Magee

REASON IN ALL THINGS

The Nurseryman, upon his knees,
Was talking to his little trees:

I heard him say: 'Now little trees
Pay close attention, if you please.
The time has come for us to part;
You're old enough to make a start,
And Lady Binks is buying you
To form a nice long avenue.

'But, little trees, remember please,
I've got to earn my bread and cheese;
And, though 'tis natural that you
Should want to show what you can do
A minor weakness, here and there,
Will not be more than I can bear.

'Kindly remember, little trees,
Although we do our best to please,
A little failure, now and then,
Appeals to all good nurserymen:
If one or two of you should fail,
Then I shall get a second sale!'

Reginald Arkell

EVERYTHING CHANGES

(*after Brecht*)

Everything changes.
        We plant
Trees for those born later –
but what's happened has happened
and poisons poured into the seas
cannot be drained out again.

What's happened has happened.
Poisons poured into the seas
cannot be drained out again
        But
Everything changes. We plant
trees for those born later.

Cicely Herbert

FOR THE FUTURE

Planting trees early in spring,
we make a place for birds to sing
in time to come. How do we know?
They are singing here now.

Wendell Berry

FINDERS-KEEPERS

The child said,
'It's an aeroplane, with a tail and wings:
Let me have it;
I'm a pilot,
I can fly to where the sky begins.'

The boy said,
'It's a sword; the blade is whittled fine:
I'm a knight,
I can fight and slay the dragon;
It should be mine.'

The girl said,
'It was I who found it;
It belongs to me:
I'll plant it;
See, the arms are branches;
They will blossom and bear leaves;
It is a tree.'

Cicely Barnes

If I keep a green bough in my heart,
   the singing bird will come.

Anon

ACKNOWLEDGEMENTS

The Editor and Publishers are grateful to the following copyright holders for permission to include copyright material in this anthology:

PAT AMICK: 'Shades of Green' from No Earthly Reason 1989, copyright the author and Commonword Ltd; to Crocus Books, Commonword Ltd, Manchester.

REGINALD ARKELL: 'Those Latin Names' from Greenfingers and 'New Sayings' 'Progress' and 'Reason in all Things' from And a Green Thumb, first published Herbert Jenkins 1934 and 1950; to Random Century Ltd.

BARBARA BAKER: 'A Spike of Green' from All Day Long, edited by Pamela Whitlock, Oxford University Press 1954; to the author.

MARJORIE BALDWIN: 'The Nature Lesson'; to the author.

GEORGE BARKER: 'Written in Surrey' from Poems of Places & People by George Barker; to Faber and Faber.

CICELY BARNES: 'Finders-Keepers'; to the author.

FRANCES BELLERBY: 'The Old Ones' from Selected Poems, Enitharmon Press 1986, copyright Charles Causley; to Charles Causley and David Higham Associates.

HILAIRE BELLOC: 'The Elm', 'His Own Country' from Complete Poems, Gerald Duckworth & Co Ltd, 1970, 1988; to the Peters Fraser and Dunlop Group Ltd.

WENDELL BERRY: 'For the Future' from Collected Poems, copyright 1984 by Wendell Berry; to North Point Press.

JOHN BETJEMAN: 'Inexpensive Progress' from Collected Poems; to John Murray (Publishers) Ltd.

JIM BURNS: 'Down by the River' from Doves for the Seventies, copyright the author 1969; to Corgi Books, Transworld.

CONOR CARSON: 'The Beech Tree' from Sea in my Mind, Puffin Books 1990; to the author.

CHARLES CAUSLEY: 'Green man in the garden' from Collected Poems, Macmillan 1975; to the author and David Higham Associates.

TONY CHEN: 'Question' from Run, Zebra, Run, Farrar, Straus and Giroux; to the author.

RICHARD CHURCH: 'Housing Scheme' from Collected Poems, William Heinemann Ltd; to the Estate of Richard Church & Laurence Pollinger Ltd.

LEONARD CLARK: 'Green Winter' from The Singing Time, Hodder & Stoughton 1980; to the Literary Executor of Leonard Clark.

FRANCES CORNFORD: 'August at Home' from On a Calm Shore, Cresset Press 1960; to the Executor, Frances Cornford Will Trust.

MARGARET CROPPER: 'I Didn't Want Anything New' from Something and Everything, Abbott Hall Art Gallery, Kendal 1980; to the Literary Executor of Margaret Cropper.

NEIL CURRY: 'Dandelion' from Ships in Bottles, Enitharmon Press 1988; to the author and Enitharmon Press.

RUTH DALLAS: 'Felled Trees' from Collected Poems, Otago University Press 1987; to the author and John McIndoe Ltd.

WALTER DE LA MARE: 'The Little Green Orchard' and 'Seeds' from Collected Poems, Faber and Faber; to the Literary Trustees of Walter de la Mare and The Society of Authors as their representative.

OLIVE DEHN: 'Song' and 'The Park'; to the author.

HELEN DUNMORE: 'The Cherry Stump' from The Raw Garden by Helen Dunmore 1988; to Bloodaxe Books Ltd.

CLIFFORD DYMENT: 'The Axe in the Wood' from Collected Poems Dent 1970; to J.M. Dent.

RICHARD EDWARDS: 'Bramble Talk' and 'Ten Tall Trees' from A Mouse in My Roof 1988; to Orchard Books and Dell Publishing. 'Who' from Whispers from a Wardrobe; to Lutterworth Press.

T.S. ELIOT: 'New Hampshire' from Collected Poems 1909–1962 Faber and Faber, copyright 1936 by Harcourt Brace Jovanovich, Inc., copyright © 1964, 1963 by T.S. Eliot; to Faber and Faber and Harcourt Brace Jovanovich Inc.

ELEANOR FARJEON: 'Trees' from Martin Pippin in the Daisy Field Oxford University Press. 'The Song of the Fir', 'To Any Garden' and 'The Tired Tree' from Silver Sand and Snow, Michael Joseph; to Gervase Farjeon as Literary Executor of the Eleanor Farjeon Estate.

ROBERT FROST: 'In Hardwood Groves' and 'Tree at my Window' from The Poetry of Robert Frost edited by Edward Connery Lathem (Jonathan Cape). Copyright © 1928, 1934, 1969 by Holt Rinehart and Winston. Copyright © 1956, 1962 by Robert Frost; to the Estate of Robert Frost and Henry Holt and Company Inc.

KATHERINE GALLAGHER: 'Tree-Planting (for Julien)' from Fish-Rings on Water, Forest Books, London 1989, copyright Katherine Gallagher; to the author.

VIRGINIA GRAHAM: 'Spring Song'; to the author.

BRYAN GUINNESS: 'The Stricken Magnolia' from The Rose in the Tree, Heinemann 1965; to the author.

JOHN HEATH-STUBBS: 'The Green Woodpecker' 'The Greenfinch', 'The Wood Warbler, the Willow Warbler & the Chiff-chaff' from A Parliament of Birds, Chatto and Windus 1975; to David Higham Associates.

A.P. HERBERT: 'Greenfly, it's difficult to see'; to A.P. Watt on behalf of the Executors.

CHARLES REZNIKOFF: 'Traffic Light' from *The Waters of Manhattan* by Charles Reznikoff, copyright © 1927 Charles Reznikoff, copyright © 1934 the Objectivist Press, copyright © 1962 by New Directions; to New Directions Publishing Company, New York.

THEODORE ROETHKE: 'Transplanting' from *Collected Poems of Theodore Roethke*, copyright © 1948 Theodore Roethke; to Doubleday, a division of Bantam Doubleday, Dell Publishing Group Inc. and Faber and Faber.

CLIVE SANSOM: 'Summer Hedgerow' from *Dorset Village*, Methuen, 'The Poem I'd Like to Write', 'Tree' and 'Magic' from *An English Year*, Chatto and Windus; to David Higham Associates.

JAMES SCHUYLER: 'I Think' and 'Sunday' from *Hymn to Life*; to Farrar, Straus and Giroux.

IAN SERRAILLIER: 'Weeping Willow in My Garden' from *I'll Tell You a Tale*, Longman 1973; to the author.

MATT SIMPSON: 'Knowing Where to Look', copyright © Matt Simpson 1990; to the author.

STEVIE SMITH: 'I Love' and 'The Pleasures of Friendship' from *Collected Poems of Stevie Smith*, copyright © 1972 Stevie Smith; to New Directions Publishing Corporation and James MacGibbon, Literary Executor.

JAMES STEPHENS: 'When You Walk' and 'The Rivals' from *Collected Poems*, Macmillan 1926; to the Society of Authors on behalf of the copyright owner, Mrs Iris Wise.

SEAN STREET: 'The Leaves are Down' from *A Walk in Winter* 1989; to the author and Enitharmon Press.

HAL SUMMERS: 'Leaves in the Yard' from *Tomorrow is My Love*, copyright © 1978 Hal Summers; to the Oxford University Press.

DAVID SUTTON: 'Cool Medium' from *Absences and Celebrations*, Chatto and Windus 1982 and 'Summer Rain' and 'Two Trees' from *Out on a Limb*, Rapp and Whiting 1969; to the author and the publishers.

ANDREW TAYLOR: 'Hill Rolling' from *Wheels Around the World* edited by Chris Searle 1983; to Macdonald, Publishers.

COLIN THIELE: 'Why did they knock down the trees, Daddy?' from *Selected Poems*, Rigby Ltd, Australia 1970; to the author.

R.S. THOMAS: 'Cynddylan on a Tractor' from *Song at the Year's Turning*, Faber and Faber, copyright R.S. Thomas; to Gwydion Thomas, 53 Gloucester Rd, Kew, UK.

NICOLA TYSON: 'Nowhere to Play', first published in *Notting Hill and Ealing High School Magazine* 1972; to the author.

LOUIS UNTERMEYER: 'To a Telegraph Pole' from *Burning Bush*, copyright © 1928 and renewed 1956 by Louis Untermeyer; to Harcourt Brace Jovanovich Inc.

JOHN WALSH: 'Ann's Flowers' from *The Roundabout by the Sea* Oxford University Press 1960; to Mrs. A.M. Walsh.

HERBERT WILLIAMS: 'A Celebration' from *Herbert Williams: Corgi Modern Poets in Focus 1*. Edited by Dannie Abse 1971.

VALERIE WORTH: 'Frog' and 'Grass' from *Small Poems* by Valerie Worth, copyright © 1972 Valerie Worth. 'Barefoot' from *Still More Small Poems* by Valerie Worth, copyright © 1976/7/8 Valerie Worth; to Farrar, Straus and Giroux Inc.

JUDITH WRIGHT: 'Rainforest' from *Phantom Dwelling*, copyright © Judith Wright; to Virago Press and Collins Angus and Robertson.

KIT WRIGHT: 'Acorn Haiku' from *Cat among the Pigeons*, Kestrel 1987; to the author.

YI-HWANG: 'Why are the green hills always so green?' from *Love in Midwinter Night*; to Kegan Paul International, London.

Quotation in the dedication comes from *So Which is the Truth* by Molly Holden, published by Carcanet.

The Editor and Publishers have made every effort to trace the holders of copyright in all poems included in this anthology. If, however, any query should arise, it should be addressed to the Publishers.

INDEX OF POETS AND TITLES

190

INDEX OF FIRST LINES

191